Alfred Tennyson
An Annotated
Bibliography

Alfred Tennyson
An Annotated
Bibliography

By

CHARLES TENNYSON

and

CHRISTINE FALL

UNIVERSITY OF GEORGIA PRESS

ATHENS

Copyright © 1967 by
University of Georgia Press

Library of Congress Catalog Card Number: 67-20677

Printed in the United States of America

Contents

	PREFACE	vii
1.	BIOGRAPHICAL	1
2.	ARTHUR HENRY HALLAM	12
3.	HOMES AND HAUNTS	13
4.	RELIGION, PHILOSOPHY, ETHICS	15
5.	TENNYSON AND SCIENCE	21
6.	POEMS NOT INCLUDED IN THE COLLECTED EDITION	25
7.	ANNOTATED EDITIONS AND SELECTIONS	27
8.	SOURCES	31
9.	BIOGRAPHIES, CONCORDANCES, HANDBOOKS	34
10.	CRITICAL AND INTERPRETATIVE: GENERAL	39
11.	CRITICAL AND INTERPRETATIVE: SPECIFIC VOLUMES AND MAJOR POEMS	67
12.	CRITICAL AND INTERPRETATIVE: SHORTER POEMS	85
13.	TENNYSON AND THE REVIEWERS	94
14.	THE DRAMAS	96
	Queen Mary	99
	Harold	104
	Becket	107
	The Cup and *The Falcon*	114
	The Promise of May	119
	The Foresters	121

Preface

THE aim of this volume is to assist research regarding the life and work of Tennyson. Elementary and introductory materials have, therefore, not been included. Nor have we attempted any bibliography of Tennyson's publications, although we have tried to cover important annotated editions, volumes of selections with valuable editorial matter, and poems and fragments not included in the collected editions. We have made no attempt to deal with any but English language publications. With these exceptions we have endeavoured to list all material, in book or periodical form, of substantial biographical, interpretative, or critical value, and to indicate by brief notes the nature of each item listed. We have not attempted a detailed survey of contemporary press and magazine reviews of the poems. The British reviews up to 1859 are well covered in Professor Edgar F. Shannon's *Tennyson and the Reviewers* (Harvard University Press, 1952) and "The Critical Reception of Tennyson's 'Maud,'" *PMLA*, LXVIII (1953), 397-414, and Joyce Green's "Tennyson's Development During the 'Ten Years' Silence' (1832-1842)," *PMLA*, LXVI (1951), 662-697, while the American reviews for the same period are well covered by Professor John O. Eidson in his *Tennyson in America* (University of Georgia Press, 1943). After 1859 the press coverage was so extensive that it could not be adequately surveyed in a volume of this size. We have, however, referred to a few of the most influential reviews which appeared at different stages of Tennyson's long career, and we have made a fairly full reference to press reviews and criticisms of Tennyson's dramas, both those relating to the publications in book form and those dealing with stage productions. We have thought this desirable owing to the relatively small amount of literature dealing with the dramas and because of the special status of stage production, which, in spite of the great importance of production values, is hardly dealt with at all except in the contemporary press.

The material is printed under headings, a list of which is given in the "Contents," and indexed in alphabetical order under the surnames of the authors. We hope this arrangement will prove useful to students. Each entry is briefly annotated to give a rough idea of its scope and value.

Complete coverage is not claimed for our bibliography. Our aim has been a near-literary presentation of selected material which may have some interest for the general reader as well as value for research.

Charles Tennyson
Christine Fall

1

Biographical

Allingham, William. *A Diary*, ed. H. Allingham and D. Radford. London: Macmillan, 1907.
    Allingham, a minor poet of merit, was a close friend of Tennyson. His diary contains much relevant material of value.

Austin, Alfred. "Tennyson's Literary Sensitiveness," *National Review*, XX (December 1892), 454-460.
    Interesting account of talks with Tennyson by his successor as Poet Laureate. Maintains that his literary sensitiveness arose from a simplicity of temperament and naivety of character, absolutely and beautifully childlike.

Benson, Arthur Christopher. *Alfred Tennyson*. New York: Dutton, 1904. London: Methuen and Co., 1904.
    Benson states as his objects (1) to give narrative of Tennyson's life, (2) to present Tennyson's view of the poet's life and character, (3) to touch on chief technical characteristics.

Brookfield, Charles and Frances. *Mrs. Brookfield and her Circle*. 2 vols. London: Sir Isaac Pitman and Sons, 1905.
    Contains interesting material regarding Tennyson's Cambridge circle, with many references to Tennyson himself. W. H. Brookfield ("old Brooks") was one of Tennyson's best loved friends. The account of him and his wife here given should be supplemented by a study of Gordon Ray's *Life of Thackeray*.

Brookfield, Frances M. *The Cambridge "Apostles"*. London: Sir Isaac Pitman, 1906.
    Contains accounts of twelve "Apostles," including Tennyson and Arthur Hallam, based on letters, family tradition, and "literary records." The authoress was the wife of Charles Brookfield, son of W. H. Brookfield. Her accounts are valuable owing to the sources from which they derive, but her statements require checking.

Brookfield, Mrs. W. H. "Early Recollections of Tennyson," *Temple Bar*, CI (February 1894), 203-207.

Characteristic reminiscences by the widow of one of Tennyson's closest friends.

Brown, Alan Willard. *The Metaphysical Society: Victorian Minds in Crisis, 1869-1880.* New York: Columbia University Press, 1947.

A history of the Metaphysical Society, of which Tennyson was one of the founders, and a study of the nineteenth century conflict between science and religion. Chapter I, pp. 1-9, is an interesting presentation of the Cambridge "Apostles" as the model and the spirit of the Metaphysical Society. Chapter II, pp. 10-19, gives an interesting account of the friendship of Tennyson with Sir James Knowles.

Chapman, Elizabeth Rachel. "Talks with Tennyson," Part I, *Putnam's Magazine*, VII (February 1910), 546-552.

An excellent article by the author of the analysis of *In Memoriam* which was approved by the poet. The talks she describes were on pertinent subjects and contain worthwhile statements. She sums up the impressions of the first meeting: "his kindliness, his humour, and his simplicity." An interesting comment of Browning, p. 549.

Chapman, Elizabeth Rachel. "Talks with Tennyson," Part II, *Putnam's Magazine*, VII (March 1910), 746-752.

In this article Tennyson is quoted as saying that *none* of his poems are about himself. There are interesting remarks about the attitude of English people towards poetry. The talks continue on a high level of subject matter.

Chesterton, G. K. and Richard Garnett. *Tennyson.* London: Hodder and Stoughton, 1903.

One of the series of "Bookman Biographies." Very fully and excellently illustrated. Short and popular in form but worth study as the work of two first-class minds.

Cornish, Mrs. Warre. "Memories of Tennyson," *The London Mercury*, V (December 1921), 144-155; (January 1922), 266-275.

Personal recollections, interesting and valuable.

Cuthbertson, Evan J. *Tennyson: The Story of His Life.* London and Edinburgh: W. and R. Chambers, 1898.

128 octavo pages, based on Hallam Tennyson's memoir.

BIOGRAPHICAL 3

Dodgson, Charles L. (Lewis Carroll). "A Visit to Tennyson," *Strand Magazine*, XXI (May 1901), 543-544.
A very interesting letter from "Lewis Carroll" to his cousin, telling of a visit to Farringford.

Fuller, Hester Thackeray. *Three Freshwater Friends: Tennyson, Watts, and Mrs. Cameron*. Newport, Isle of Wight: The County Press, 1933.
The authoress, grand-daughter of Thackeray and daughter of Anne Thackeray Ritchie, here tries to recreate "the Freshwater which Tennyson knew and loved and which, for all time, holds a very remarkable place in literary history."

Gernsheim, Helmut. *Julia Margaret Cameron*. London: Fountain Press, 1948.
Remarkable photographs, including many of Tennyson and his circle. Mrs. Cameron's life and her early and artistic use of a new mechanical medium are of great interest. Her subjects are a history of her time. Mrs. Cameron was a neighbour and close friend of Tennyson on the Isle of Wight in the 1860's and early 1870's. (See also under V. Scott O'Connor.)

Gosse, Sir Edmund. "A First Sight of Tennyson," in *Selected Essays* (First Series). London: Heinemann, 1928.
A vivid description of a young man's first meeting with Tennyson in the British Museum, at the height of his fame. It is said that the "famous black bust of Antinous" referred to cannot be identified.

Graham, P. Anderson. "Lord Tennyson's Childhood," *The Art Journal*, XV (1891), 13-18, 46-50.
Biographical value small, as later publications have absorbed or superseded it. Some valuable illustrations.

Horton, Robert Forman. *Alfred Tennyson: a Saintly Life*. London: J. M. Dent, 1900.
The title explains the approach. The biography is an abridgement of facts in *The Memoir* plus Horton's inferences, which are all favourable.

Houghton, Walter E. *The Victorian Frame of Mind: 1830-1870*. New Haven: Yale University Press, 1957.
An important work for background study.

Howe, M. A. de W. "The Tennysons at Farringford: A Victorian Vista. Drawn from the Unpublished Papers of Mrs.

James T. Fields," *Cornhill Magazine*, N. S., LXIII (October 1927), 447-457.
    Describes visits by James T. Fields, Tennyson's American publisher, and his wife to Tennyson at Farringford. The descriptions have value as immediate records of experience.

Howe, M. A. de W. "The Late Alfred Baron Tennyson, Poet Laureate," *The Illustrated London News*, October 13, 1892, pp. 483-492.
    Important for photographs not usually seen, such as the poet in his velvet skull-cap by Cameron and Smith; meeting of Tennyson and Garibaldi in 1864, drawn by Sir John Gilbert; and pictures of the poet's sons.

Jennings, Henry J. *Lord Tennyson, a Biographical Sketch*. London: Chatto and Windus, 1884. Revised and enlarged edition, 1892.
    Compiled during Tennyson's life, mostly from the rather scanty published resources then available. The author in the Preface to the second edition claims to have submitted his script to a near member of the Tennyson family. The book has little value today.

Johnson, Reginald Brimley. *Tennyson and His Poetry*. London: Harrap, 1917.
    Life story of the poet, with emphasis on his personality as it expressed itself in his poetry.

Knight, William. "A Reminiscence of Tennyson," *Blackwood's Magazine*, CLXII (August 1897), 264-270.
    A valuable account of a visit to Tennyson at Farringford in May 1890, by a professor at the University of St. Andrews, whom the poet evidently found very congenial. Does not seem to have been used by biographers—worth study.

Knowles, James. "Aspects of Tennyson. A Personal Reminiscence," *Nineteenth Century*, XXXIII (January 1893), 164-188.
    A valuable chapter of reminiscences by Tennyson's close friend, the editor of the review. One of a series of special obituary articles.

Lincolnshire Archives Committee. Archivists' Reports for 1949-1950, 1950-1951, 1960-1961.
    Describe deposits of documents relating to the history of the Tennyson family during the 18th and early 19th centuries.

Long, Mason. "The Tennysons and the Brownings," *College English*, IX (December 1947), 131-139.
A useful synthesis of the published material regarding the personal relations of these poets.

Lounsbury, Thomas Raynesford. *The Life and Times of Tennyson from 1809-1850.* New Haven: Yale University Press, 1915. London: Oxford University Press, 1915.
A basic book, supplementing the *Memoir* by Hallam Tennyson. Today some scholars consider certain conclusions lacking in accuracy. Unfortunately Professor Lounsbury died before he could give his text the final revision.

Lyall, Sir Alfred Comyns. *Tennyson.* English Men of Letters Series. London: Macmillan, 1902. Reprinted 1905, 1907, 1910, 1914.
An excellent short biography by a close friend of the poet, with running commentary on the poems, as they illustrate Tennyson's intellectual habits and the circumstances of his life.

Macnaughton, G.F.A. *Tennyson: an Interview.* Glasgow: R. Maclehose and Co., 1929.
Describes a visit to Tennyson at Farringford with the object of persuading him to stand for the Lord Rectorship of Glasgow University, and its consequences.

McCabe, W. Gordon. "Personal Recollections of Alfred, Lord Tennyson," *Century Magazine*, LXIII (March 1902), 722-737.
An entertaining record by an American admirer who visited Tennyson several times during the last years of his life and was much liked by him.

Miller, Betty. "Tennyson: The Early Years," *Twentieth Century*, CLXVII (June 1960), 520-529.
The principal value of this sketch is its emphasis on the Gothic influences upon Tennyson's early years. Mrs. Miller finds the Gothic background "perfectly adapted, alike to the emotional needs and the emotional limitations, of this remarkable Victorian personality."

Nemo. "Tennysoniana. By one who knew the late Lord Tennyson," *Sunday Magazine* (January 1893), 50-53; (February 1893), 122-125; (March 1893), 201-205.
The writer evidently knew Tennyson well, and the papers have biographical value.

Noel, Roden. "Lord Tennyson, with a Few Personal Reminiscences," *Atlanta Magazine* (1892), 264.

A survey by a poet of whose work Tennyson thought well. The personal reminiscences have more value today than the criticism.

O'Connor, V. Scott. "Mrs. Cameron, Her Friends and Her Photographs," *Century Magazine*, LV (November 1897), 3-10, 240-268.

A short article founded on material supplied by Mrs. Cameron's son. (See also under Gernsheim, above.) Mrs. Cameron was for many years a close friend of Tennyson and made many portraits of him and his family.

Parsons, Eugene. *Tennyson's Life and Poetry: and Mistakes Concerning Tennyson*. Chicago: Gray Press, 1892, 1893.

An exposure of "misleading and conflicting statements" found in "articles on Tennyson in cyclopedias and biographical dictionaries." Short biographical sketch. Appendix of translations of Tennyson's works into various languages.

Pierce, Lorne. *Alfred Lord Tennyson and William Kirby*. Toronto: Macmillan, 1929.

Correspondence between Tennyson and a Canadian loyalist showing the poet's strong belief in the destiny of the British Empire and his eager desire for a "seamless union" between Britain and her colonies.

Rader, Ralph Wilson. "Tennyson and Rosa Baring," *Victorian Studies*, V (March 1962), 224-260.

A convincing presentation of facts concerning the poet's early love for Rosa Baring and its effect upon his art. The essay appears as Chapter II of Rader's *Tennyson's "Maud": The Biographical Genesis*.

Rader, Ralph Wilson. "Tennyson in the Year of Hallam's Death," *PMLA*, LXXVII (September 1962), 419-424.

"The record . . . taken up mostly with externals . . . from the diary for the years 1833-1835 of Tennyson's friend, the Rev. John Rashdall, now accessible in the Bodleian Library." Aim of essay is to give "a fuller, more detailed account than has yet been available of Tennyson in the year of Hallam's death." Does not concern any view "of the inner man." Very interesting. The essay appears as section ii of Chapter I of Rader's *Tennyson's "Maud": The Biographical Genesis*.

Rader, Ralph Wilson. *Tennyson's "Maud": The Biographical Genesis.* Berkeley: University of California Press, 1963.
    Examines Tennyson's relations with Rosa Baring, Sophy Rawnsley, and Emily Sellwood, and their effects on his poems, particularly *Maud* and the two *Locksley Halls.* Throws much new light on the composition of *Maud* and on Tennyson's friendship with Rosa Baring. Perhaps goes too far in identifying characters in the poems with actual people.

Rawnsley, Hardwicke Drummond. *Memories of the Tennysons.* Glasgow: Maclehose, 1900.
    First-hand information about the Tennyson family, Lincolnshire and its people, the poet's life at Farringford and at Aldworth. Chapter IX draws parallels between Virgil and Tennyson, and the last chapter is on the Laureate's favourite brother, Charles (Tennyson) Turner. It must be remembered in reading publications of the Rawnsleys that they were much influenced by the very Victorian attitude of the poet and his son Hallam towards personal publicity. H. D. Rawnsley was a son of the Rev. D. Rawnsley, Tennyson's closest Lincolnshire friend, and knew the poet well.

Rawnsley, Willingham Franklin. *Tennyson, 1809-1909: a Lecture.* Ambleside: Middleton, 1909.
    Another son of the Rev. D. Rawnsley gives a very personal account of the Tennysons. Full of facts; has reference value. (See note on preceding item.)

Rawnsley, Willingham Franklin. "Personal Recollections of Tennyson," *The Nineteenth Century and After,* XCVII (January 1925), 1-9; (February 1925), 190-196.
    The recollections contain some good material.

Richardson, Joanna. *The Pre-eminent Victorian.* London: Jonathan Cape, 1962.
    A study of Tennyson as a great Victorian and symbol of the Victorian age. The authoress had the advantage of access to a good deal of hitherto unused or little used material.

Ritchie, Anne Thackeray. "Alfred Tennyson," *Harper's Magazine,* LXVIII (December 1883), 21-41.
    Valuable first-hand information from a daughter of W. M. Thackeray who knew Tennyson intimately. Beautiful illustrations. Reprinted in *Records of Tennyson, Ruskin, and Browning.* London: Macmillan, 1892.

Roz, Firmin. *Tennyson.* Paris: Bloud, 1911. Boston: Ginn and Co., 1911.
   A two hundred and twenty page life founded on Hallam Tennyson's *Memoir*, the Eversley edition of the poems, and the Athenaeum Press edition of the poems edited by Henry van Dyke and D. Laurance Chambers.

Sanders, Charles Richard. "Carlyle and Tennyson," *PMLA*, LXXVI (March 1961), 82-97.
   A full and interesting account of the relations between the two men.

Schonfield, Hugh J. *Letters to Frederick Tennyson.* London: Hogarth Press, 1930.
   A collection of letters from various friends and relatives to Frederick Tennyson, Alfred's eldest brother. Of considerable biographical interest. The reader should beware of misprints.

Schooling, J. Holt. "The Handwriting of Alfred, Lord Tennyson," *The Strand Magazine*, VIII (1894), 599-608.
   Reproduces a "collection of extracts from Lord Tennyson's letters," written between his 17th and 83rd years.

Shannon, Edgar F., Jr. "Alfred Tennyson's Admission to Cambridge," *Times Literary Supplement*, March 6, 1959, p. 136.
   Not only establishes the date for Tennyson's commencing his career at the university, November 1827, but also draws a number of important conclusions pertaining to the poet's life and character.

Stephen, Leslie. "Life of Tennyson," in *Studies of a Biographer*. London: Duckworth and Co., 1907.
   A long essay by one of the greatest Victorian critics, who became a freshman just after the appearance of *In Memoriam* and graduated the year before the appearance of *"Maud."* Stephen was an enthusiastic admirer of the poems of 1842 and *In Memoriam* but found himself unable to maintain an equal enthusiasm for Tennyson's later work or appreciate its allegorical and philosophic quality.

Stoker, Bram. *Personal Reminiscences of Henry Irving.* London: Heinemann, 1906.
   Stoker was Irving's "Acting Manager" and intimate friend for thirty years. This book contains exceptionally vivid and convincing recollections of Tennyson and some valuable sidelights on his merits and defects as a dramatist.

Teeling, Bartle. "A Visit to the Tennysons in 1859," *Blackwood's Magazine*, CLV (May 1894), 605-621.
 An interesting account of the Tennyson family at a date when very little is recorded of them. A full summary occurs in Sir Charles Tennyson's *Alfred Tennyson*.

Tennyson, Sir Charles. "Tennyson Papers: I. Alfred's Father," *Cornhill Magazine*, CLIII (March 1936), 283-305.
 Important material, but written without knowledge of the Bayons Manor papers. Compare with material on early life of the poet in Sir Charles Tennyson's *Alfred Tennyson*.

Tennyson, Sir Charles. "Tennyson Papers: II. J. M. Heath's 'Commonplace Book'," *Cornhill Magazine*, CLIII (April 1936), 426-449.
 Description of a MS. notebook kept by a contemporary and friend of Tennyson at Cambridge, now in the Fitzwilliam Museum, Cambridge.

Tennyson, Sir Charles. *Alfred Tennyson*. London: Macmillan, 1949.
 The most complete biography, contains much new material concerning the poet's early years, mostly drawn from family correspondence dating between 1800 and 1850, and preserved at Bayons Manor, Lincolnshire, now in the Lincolnshire County Archives, the Castle, Lincoln, England.

Tennyson, Sir Charles. "The Tennyson Phonograph Records," *Bulletin of the British Institute of Recorded Sound*. No. 3 (Winter 1965), pp. 2-8.
 A note on the phonograph recordings of Tennyson's reading his own poems made during the years 1890-1892.

Tennyson, Sir Charles. "Tennyson's Conversation," *The Twentieth Century*, CLXV (January 1959), 34-44.
 Based on notes kept of conversations with his father by the poet's eldest son when a schoolboy and undergraduate.

Tennyson, Sir Charles. "The Somersby Tennysons," *Victorian Studies*, Christmas Supplement, 1963.
 Brings together for the first time important details of the lives of Tennyson's brothers and sisters, indirectly throwing a good deal of light on the life and character of Tennyson himself.

Tennyson, Sir Charles. "Tennyson and His Times," *Lincolnshire Historian*, II, No. 11 (1964).

Brief summary of references in Tennyson's work to the political events of his time.

Tennyson, Hallam Lord. *Alfred, Lord Tennyson, A Memoir.* 2 vols. London: Macmillan, 1897.

Basic source book for study of Tennyson: dates, letters, notes, quotations from manuscripts, unpublished poems, journal of the Tennyson home life, anecdotes, reviews are given with little comment. "Final authority on points it deals with," says Lounsbury. But some inaccuracies have been pointed out by later writers. Issued in a single volume by the same publishers in 1899.

Tennyson, Hallam Lord, ed. *Tennyson and His Friends.* London: Macmillan, 1911.

Very valuable reference material. Companion book to Hallam, Lord Tennyson's *Memoir.* (See preceding item.)

Terry, Ellen. *The Story of My Life.* London: Hutchinson and Co., 1908.

Contains some delightful and vivid recollections of Tennyson and of Irving's production of *The Cup* which the authoress calls "a beautiful tragedy," surpassing *Becket* in "sheer poetic intensity," though "not nearly so good a play."

Swinburne, A. C. "Threnody. Alfred, Lord Tennyson, October 6, 1892," *Nineteenth Century,* XXXIII (January 1893), 1-3.

Evidence of Swinburne's genuine admiration for Tennyson.

Tryon, W. S. "Nationalism and International Copyright: Tennyson and Longfellow in America," *American Literature,* XXIV (November 1952), 301-309.

An interesting analysis of Tennyson's sales in America compared with Longfellow's. Much the most successful book by either poet was *Enoch Arden. Hiawatha* came second but with a considerable interval.

Vail Motter, T. H. "When Did Tennyson Meet Hallam?" *Modern Language Notes,* LVII (March 1942), 209.

Argues, chiefly from the evidence of *In Memoriam* XXII and XLVI, that Tennyson and Arthur Hallam first met in April 1829 and not in the Autumn of 1828 as previously stated.

Vail Motter, T. H. *The Writings of Arthur Hallam.* New York: Modern Language Association of America, 1943. London: Oxford University Press, 1943.

Essential reading for the Tennyson student. Includes a useful bibliography.

Ward, Wilfrid. *Problems and Persons.* London: Longmans Green, 1903.

Chapter VI, "Tennyson," is one of the best contemporary descriptions of Tennyson in middle and old age. Wilfrid Ward was a son of Tennyson's friend W. G. Ward, and himself a friend of Tennyson's sons. He developed into a noted Catholic scholar and biographer.

Ward, Wilfrid. *Men and Matters.* London: Longmans Green, 1914.

Chapter VII contains another admirable sketch of Tennyson and his Farringford circle by the son of his friend, W. G. Ward.

Watson, Aaron. *Tennyson.* London: T. C. and E. C. Jack. New York: Dodge Publishing Co., n. d.

A short biography founded on Hallam Tennyson's *Memoir* and useful as an introduction.

Watts, Theodore. "The Portraits of Lord Tennyson," *The Magazine of Art,* XVI (December 1892), 37-43; (January 1893), 96-101.

An excellent collection of portraits with useful biographical notes by a personal friend of the poet.

Waugh, Arthur. *Alfred Lord Tennyson: a Study of his Life and Works.* London: Heinemann, 1902. First edition 1892.

Chronological treatment of the life of the poet, with a great deal of commentary on the poems. The most substantial life written before Hallam Tennyson's *Memoir.*

Weld, Agnes Grace. *Glimpses of Tennyson and Some of his Relations and Friends.* London: Williams and Norgate, 1903.

Agnes Weld, niece of Emily, Lady Tennyson, writes of the Tennysons and Sellwoods. Biographical value lies in her personal knowledge. Appendix contains a note on Bertram Tennyson, son of Horatio Tennyson, the poet's brother, with reprint of a short story and poem by him. For Bertram Tennyson see also *The Somersby Tennysons* by Sir Charles Tennyson, above.

White, Walter. *Journals.* London: Chapman and Hall, 1898.

Contains on pp. 141-168 reminiscences of Tennyson during the years 1845-1878.

Arthur Henry Hallam

Arthur Hallam's writings in prose and verse were admirably collected and edited by T. H. Vail Motter in his *The Writings of Arthur Hallam* (New York: Modern Language Association of America, 1943. London: Oxford University Press, 1943). This contains, in Appendix B, an excellent note on the critical literature and in Appendix C a note as to the printed collections of Hallam's letters. To these records can be added *An Eton Boy*, edited by Charles Milnes Gaskell (London: Constable and Company, 1939); and "Some Unpublished Poems by Arthur Henry Hallam," edited by Sir Charles Tennyson and F. T. Baker, *Victorian Poetry*, III, No. 3, Supplement (Summer 1965), 1-18, a publication of the Tennyson Society.

Hallam's friendship with Tennyson is of course dealt with in all the lives of Tennyson. Earlier authorities are as follows:

Remains in Verse and Prose of A. H. H., ed. with a preface by his father, Henry Hallam. Privately printed, London, 1834. Reprinted privately with a memoir of A. H. H.'s brother, Henry Fitzmaurice Hallam, by Sir H. S. Maine and F. Lushington. London, 1853. The first edition was published by John Murray in London in 1862, and the second edition was similarly published in 1863.

3

Homes and Haunts

Church, Alfred. *Laureate's Country.* London: Seeley, 1891.
   According to Hallam, Lord Tennyson (*Memoir* single volume edition p. 723) this book and G. G. Napier's *The Homes and Haunts of Alfred, Lord Tennyson* (see below) were the only two topographical books concerning him which Tennyson considered at all accurate.

Francis, Beata. *The Scenery of Tennyson's Poems.* London: John and Edward Bumpus, 1893.
   Forty etchings by various artists with introduction and descriptive letter-press. An elaborate publication but not of great value.

Napier, George G. *The Homes and Haunts of Alfred, Lord Tennyson.* Glasgow: James Maclehose and Sons, 1892. (Privately printed, 1889.)
   Excellent illustrations. According to Hallam, Lord Tennyson (*Memoir* single volume edition p. 723) this book and Alfred Church's *Laureate's Country* (see above) were the only two topographical books about him which Tennyson considered at all accurate.

O'Connor, V. Scott. "Tennyson and his Friends at Freshwater," *Century Magazine*, LV (December 1897), 240-268.
   The author was a friend of Tennyson's brother Arthur and evidently knew the locality well. This gives his article biographical value. Some good illustrations.

Paterson, Arthur. *The Homes of Tennyson.* London: Adam and Charles Black, 1905.
   Illustrations by Helen Allingham, described by Arthur Paterson. Twenty full-page illustrations. Text written from a personal rather than a biographical standpoint, giving interesting details concerning the life at Farringford and Aldworth. Helen Allingham was the wife of William Allingham, poet and diarist, a close friend of Tennyson.

Rawnsley, Drummond. "Lincolnshire Scenery and Character as Illustrated by Mr. Tennyson," *Macmillan's Magazine*, XXIX (November 1873-April 1874), 140.

Rawnsley was a close friend of Tennyson from Lincolnshire days.

Rawnsley, Hardwicke Drummond. *Homes and Haunts of Famous Authors*. London: Darton and Co., 1906.

A volume of essays by various authors including one of thirteen pages on Somersby, Farringford, and Aldworth by H. D. Rawnsley. Slight but of some value as Rawnsley knew all three homes.

Tennyson, Sir Charles. "Alfred Tennyson and Somersby," *Tennyson Chronicle*, X, No. 12 (August 1959). (A. Dunn, printer, Alford, Lincolnshire.)

Founded largely on family correspondence and local tradition. Has biographical value.

Walters, J. C. *In Tennyson Land*. A brief account of the Home and Early surroundings of the poet and an attempt to identify the scenes and trace the influence of Lincolnshire in his works. London: George Medway, 1890.

The result of local research made by the author during a holiday in Lincolnshire. Where possible, descriptions of scenery and allusions to persons and customs are made in the poet's own words.

Young, Andrew. *The Poet and the Landscape*. London: Rupert Hart-Davis, 1962.

The last essay, "Tennyson in Lincolnshire," is an agreeable if cursory disquisition by a poet of distinction.

4

Religion, Philosophy, Ethics

Note: Many studies on these subjects will be found under the headings "Critical and Interpretative, General," "In Memoriam," and "Idylls of the King."

Atkins, Gaius Glenn. *Reinspecting Victorian Religion.* New York: Macmillan, 1928.
   Treats the themes of the entangled soul in *Idylls of the King*, and faith and doubt in *In Memoriam*. Rather discursive, lacks both organization and depth, but worth study.

Auld, William Muir. *The Mount of Vision.* New York: Macmillan, 1932.
   Discusses Tennyson's spiritual teaching with special reference to *The Ancient Sage*.

Barnes, C. W. "The Faith of Tennyson," *Methodist Review*, LXXXII (July/August 1900), 582-591.
   A careful summary, interesting as showing the congeniality of Tennyson's thought to the non-dogmatic Christianity of the 19th century.

Birney, L. J. "What Tennyson Did for the Ministers," *Methodist Review*, XCIX (January/February 1917), 22-35.
   A closely reasoned statement by a sincere and cultured minister leads to this summary: "To know well this poet's mind and spirit is to be inspired to breadth and charity for every honest view, passionate purpose to know the truth and make it serve life, growing certainty of the great essentials of the faith."

Brooks, F. T. *Alfred, Lord Tennyson, a Modern Sage.* Madras: Vyasashrama Book Shop, 1914.
   From the standpoint of theosophy.

Carpenter, William Boyd. *The Message of Tennyson.* London: Macmillan, 1893.

A sermon preached in Westminster Abbey on April 30, 1893, by the Bishop of Ripon, a personal friend of the poet.

Dhruva, A. B. *Kant and Tennyson and Kant and Browning.* Bombay: The Time Press, 1917. Two lectures delivered at Ahmadabad under the auspices of the Gujarat College Library and Debating Society.

Mr. Dhruva gives an introductory outline of Kant's main philosophical ideas. His fitting Tennyson passages into the Kantian frame is interesting and to a degree successful. His categories are as follows:
  1. Subjectivity of Time and Space.
  2. Knowledge and Faith.
  3. Proofs of the Existence of God.
  4. Doctrine of Immortality.
  5. A Few Categories from the *Practical Reason.*
  6. Freedom of the Will.

Earle, John Charles. "Tennyson's Influence on the Formation of Christian Character," *The Christian Apologist,* (January 1877), 163-174.

Sincere and thoughtful and calls attention to elements of lasting value which the modern mind is apt to overlook. An interesting estimate of Tennyson's position in regard to revealed religion by a Victorian Christian theologian.

Gordon, William Clark. *The Social Ideal of Alfred Tennyson as Related to His Time.* Chicago: University of Chicago Press, 1906. London: T. Fisher Unwin, 1906.

A union of sociology and literature, giving Tennyson's idea of man, the place of woman, the family, society, and social institutions. Tennyson portrays with clearness the beauty and power of his age. His solution for the social problems is by means of the power of an ideal.

Hardwick, J. C. "Tennyson's Religion," *Modern Churchman,* XXXIX (December 1949), 317-329.

An examination of Tennyson's religious beliefs as related to his life as a whole. Does not delve deep, but suggests approaches which could be made.

Heraud, Edith. *Lecture on Tennyson.* London: Marshall and Co., 1878.

A synopsis of the moral and religious tendencies of Tennyson's poems from the point of view of the Unity Church.

Jones, Sir Henry. *The Immortality of the Soul in Tennyson and Browning*. Boston: American Unitarian Association, 1907. London: 5 Essex Street, Strand, W. C., 1906. First edition, 1905.
 A brilliant address which argues that the scientist's conception of a natural order and the idealist's conception of God are both hypotheses, one as true as the other.

Lyttleton, Arthur. "Tennyson," in *Modern Poets of Faith, Doubt and Paganism*. London: John Murray, 1904.
 A full and intelligent study of Tennyson's poetry written in 1893 by a cultured aristocratic churchman.

Masterman, C. F. G. *Tennyson as a Religious Teacher*. London: Methuen, 1900.
 Written from the point of view of an intellectual Anglican Churchman. Still the best book on Tennyson's religious thought.

Myers, F. W. H. "Modern Poets and the Meaning of Life," *Nineteenth Century*, XXXIII (January 1893), 93-111.
 A brief but important reference to Tennyson with whom Myers was intimate during the last years of his life.

Myers, Frederick W. H. "Tennyson as Prophet," *The Nineteenth Century*, XXV (March 1889), 381-396. Reprinted in *Science and a Future Life*. London: Macmillan, 1893.
 The theme is developed step by step by chronological presentation of the poems, from *Supposed Confessions* to the *Higher Pantheism*, which Myers calls Tennyson's nearest approach to a creed. Myers was a distinguished Victorian poet and psychologist. In this important essay he foresees that "if indeed the Cosmos make for good, and evolution be a moral as well as a material law," mankind may look back on Tennyson as "a leader who in the darkest hour of the world's thought could not despair of the destiny of man."

Osmond, Percy Herbert. *The Mystical Poets of the English Church*. London: Society for Promoting Christian Knowledge, 1919.
 Chapter IX is on Wordsworth, Coleridge, Tennyson, and others. Pp. 305 ff. state that Tennyson's mysticism came clearly only in his old age, but was strong from the first. Gives brief comments on the "Holy Grail," *Poems of 1842*, "The Voyage," "Merlin and the Gleam," "Sir Galahad," "Flower in the Crannied Wall," "Higher Pantheism," "De

Profundis," "Two Voices," "Crossing the Bar," *In Memoriam*, "Ancient Sage," and "Far, Far Away."

Peake, L. S. "Tennyson and the Search for Immortality," *Saturday Review*, February 20, 27, and March 12, 1932, pp. 216-217 and 266.

 A useful summary. The first article emphasizes Tennyson's belief in the pre-existence of the human soul in the spiritual world.

Robertson, John Mackinnon. *Browning and Tennyson as Teachers*. London: A. and H. B. Brown, 1903.

 Two separate studies, "Tennyson," pp. 1-83. The work of a leading free-thinker of considerable intellectual power. The lack of sympathy with Tennyson's character and point of view reduces its value as criticism.

Salt, Henry S. *Tennyson as Thinker*. London: William Reeves, 1893.

 A detailed study which comes to the conclusion that Tennyson's social philosophy is "that of a man who, by the conditions of his birth, education, temperament, and general surroundings was quite incapacitated for recognizing the progressive and intellectual tendencies of the age in which he lived."

Sinnett, Alfred P. *Tennyson, an Occultist*. London: Theosophical Publishing House, 1920.

 Written from the theosophical point of view, the book aims to show that Tennyson "was an occultist as well as a genius."

Sneath, Elias Hershey. *The Mind of Tennyson: His Thoughts on God, Freedom, and Immortality*. Westminster: Constable, 1900.

 Tennyson's thoughts on God, freedom, and immortality, interpreted in the light of his relation to the spirit of his age. Very good.

Sonn, C. R. "Poetic Vision and Religious Certainty in Tennyson's Early Poetry," *Modern Philology*, LVII (November 1959), 83-93.

 Religious impulse and aesthetic impulse are not antagonistic in Tennyson's poetry but go hand in hand.

Starnes, D. T. "The Influence of Carlyle upon Tennyson," *The Texas Review*, VI (July 1921), 316-336.

RELIGION, PHILOSOPHY, ETHICS

Stevenson, Lionel. *Darwin Among the Poets.* Chicago: University of Chicago Press, 1932.
Chapter II, "Tennyson," pp. 55-117, traces Tennyson's early struggle with doubt, his continuous study of science, the theory of evolution in *The Princess* twelve years before *The Origin of Species,* Tennyson's rejection of the purely physical in Darwin's theory, his imperative need for belief in personal survival after death, his rejection of pure materialism, and finally his synthesis of evolution and mysticism to produce faith.

Stuart, Charles M., ed. *The Vision of Christ in the Poets.* New York: Eaton and Mains, 1896.
"Alfred Tennyson," pp. 153-217. Notes, pp. 296-302. Short introduction, p. 153.

Tollemache, Lionel A. "Mr. Tennyson's Social Philosophy," *Fortnightly Review,* XXI, O.S. (February 1874), 225-247.
Finds Tennyson's writings on theology cautious and his ethical remarks mostly commonplace and attaching too much importance to domestic morality, but admits that Tennyson has helped to rid his countrymen of their hereditary intolerance and has taught morality in its purest form in every educated household.

Turner, Paul. "The Stupidest English Poet," *English Studies,* XXX (February 1949), 1-12.
A well reasoned and supported attack on those who, like Nicolson, Fausset, and Auden, belittle Tennyson's intellectual ability and courage. Finds that Tennyson's attitude and methods of thought were never unworthy of a philosopher and that he "never fought a dishonourable rear-guard action against the advance of science." A valuable essay.

Walters, J. Cuming. *Tennyson, Poet, Philosopher, Idealist.* London: Kegan Paul, 1893.
Each chapter is a separate study of some phase of Tennyson's works, with stress upon religion, philosophy, and politics. "Trifles, such as his smoking, his hats, his beer and wine are left to others."

Weatherhead, Leslie D. *The Afterworld of the Poets.* London: Epworth Press, J. Alfred Sharp, 1929.
Chapter III contains an elaborate study of Tennyson's views about the possibility of life after death. "All the main

positions taken up in modern theology with regard to the subject of eschatology may be found in *In Memoriam*, written three quarters of a century ago."

Weld, A. G. *Tennyson's Religious Life and Teachings*. Louisville, Kentucky: Baptist World Publishing Co., 1909.

    Miss Weld was Emily, Lady Tennyson's niece. Rather conventional approach, but has value owing to the writer's personal knowledge of the poet.

Wickham, E. C. *The Religious Value of Tennyson's Poetry*. Lincoln: Lincoln Cathedral, 1909.

    A sermon preached in the Cathedral on September 22, 1909, during the Tennyson Centenary Celebrations.

5

Tennyson and Science

Beach, Joseph Warren. *The Concept of Nature in Nineteenth Century English Poetry.* New York: Macmillan, 1936.
Chapter XV, "Tennyson," should be read with Lionel Stevenson's chapter in *Darwin Among the Poets.* Beach emphasizes the difference between Tennyson's position and that of Wordsworth. Though a notable "landscape painter" and student of natural science, he derived emotional impetus mainly from setting himself against nature and combating her claims in the interest of religion—or the spiritual reality.

Burroughs, John. "Whitman's and Tennyson's Relations to Science," *The Dial,* March 16, 1893, pp. 168-169.
Considers Whitman and Tennyson the only contemporary poets who have drawn inspiration from modern science, or viewed the universe through the vistas opened by science. Tennyson drew upon science for image and illustration more than Whitman, but did not so much absorb and appropriate its results.

Bush, Douglas. *Science and English Poetry.* New York: Oxford University Press, 1956.
Chapter V, "Evolution and the Victorian Poets," contains interesting references to Tennyson's position: "Although Tennyson was a closer student of science than other poets, his concern was with man and God rather than with scientific theories."

Crum, Ralph B. "Nature Red in Tooth and Claw," *Scientific Thought in Poetry.* New York: Columbia University Press. 1931.
The first chapter, "Science and Poetry," gives a brief but thoughtful history of the two fields from the Greeks to the twentieth century. In the chapter on Tennyson's problems, "Nature Red in Tooth and Claw," 157-190, Crum gives a good account of Tennyson's struggle with science and theology.

To reconcile a mechanical universe and a spiritual realm was not easy, but Tennyson retained his belief in God and personal immortality and also won the title, "the poet of science."

Emery, Clark. "The Background of Tennyson's 'Airy Navies'," *Isis*, XXXV, Part II (July 1944), 139-147.

A survey of the literature on the subject of human flight published before Tennyson composed *Locksley Hall*. Concludes that Tennyson may have visualized something after the fashion of 20th century aircraft, but that this cannot be proved or disproved. In either case he was only one, and a late one at that, of many prophets.

Evans, B. Ifor. *Literature and Science*. London: Allen and Unwin, 1954.

Chapter XII, pp. 72-78, deals with the middle and late 19th century and concludes that it is part of Tennyson's greatness that he defined more fully than any other poet in England the sense of fear and depression experienced by the imaginative artist in relation to biological science.

Gibson, Walker. "Behind the Veil: A Distinction Between Poetic and Scientific Language in Tennyson, Lyell, and Darwin," *Victorian Studies*, II (September 1958), 60-68.

By examining Tennyson's approach to scientific problems in terms of his grammar, the author seeks to demonstrate the difference between the poetic and the scientific statement and suggests one method by which a great Victorian poet was able to use for his own purposes the disquieting new world of science.

Hayes, J. W. *Tennyson and Scientific Theology*. London: Elliot Stock, 1919.

By a clergyman who was an associate member of the Society for Psychical Research and a student of natural science. Emphasizes that "Tennyson was a philosopher and a fellow-thinker with such men as Huxley, Darwin, Crocker, Sidgwick and Wallace." His productions were coloured by their profound thoughts, and their theories and discoveries were wrought into the web of his being, as a result "he must be judged by a very different standard from Byron, Shelley, Longfellow, or even Wordsworth." Previous editions from the same publisher in 1904 and 1909.

Lockyer, Sir Joseph Norman and Winifred Lockyer. *Tennyson as a Student and Poet of Nature*. London: Macmillan, 1910.

A classification by an eminent astronomer of "passages in Tennyson's *Works* which deal with the scientific aspects of nature." The range, abundance, and content of the quotations are clear evidence of Tennyson's extensive knowledge of science.

Luce, Morton. "Nature in Tennyson," *The Living Age*, CCLXXXVII (October 2, 1915), 156-161; (November 27, 1915), 604-611.

The October article is on birds in Tennyson's poetry; the November article is on trees. Luce says that Tennyson's presentations are done with scientific accuracy and poetic beauty: "Facts are in every instance transfigured by exquisite beauty."

Mackie, Alexander. *Nature Knowledge in Modern Poetry*. London: Longmans Green, 1906.

Reflections on Tennyson as botanist, entomologist, ornithologist, and geologist, demonstrating his indebtedness to scientific truth for new ideas in poetry.

Mooney, E. A., Jr. "A Note on Astronomy in Tennyson's 'Princess'," *Modern Language Notes*, LXIV (February 1949), 98-102.

Discusses the reference in Canto IV to the "Nebulous star" in relation to contemporary theories about the constitution of the sun.

Potter, George Reuben. "Tennyson and the Biological Theory of the Mutability of Species," *Philological Quarterly*, XVI (October 1937), 321-343.

A valuable study of Tennyson's views in relation to those of scientific thinkers before the publication of Darwin's *Origin of Species*. "Tennyson was not seeing by a mystic intuition the proofs of organic evolution that Darwin was to produce later . . . he was following, in a sane and clear-headed fashion, the most enlightened scientific thinkers of these decades . . . struggling to mould them into some satisfactory working philosophy of life."

Rutland, William R. "Tennyson and the Theory of Evolution," *Essays and Studies by Members of the English Association*, XXVI (1940), 7-29.

A brilliant essay, showing Tennyson's deep study of science and philosophy, his ability to make a synthesis of the two fields and to relate this abstract thought to the world in which he lived, and to a great degree foresee the changes which we now experience. It helps give one an understanding of Tennyson's resolution of the problem of death and immortality.

Starnes, D. T. "The Influence of Carlyle upon Tennyson," *The Texas Review*, VI (July 1921), 316-336.

Starnes' purpose is to examine (1) the personal and literary relations of Carlyle and Tennyson as revealed in their correspondence, memoirs, and biographies, (2) their works; and determine if influences are reflected. His categories are Nature, an Emblem of God; The One-ness of the Universe; Society and Government; Science-Evolution. Each of these topics is discussed, then in double column arrangement he lists parallel examples from their works.

Stevenson, Lionel. *Darwin Among the Poets*. Chicago: University of Chicago Press, 1932.

Chapter II, 55-116, "Alfred Tennyson," contains the most exhaustive study yet made of Tennyson's attitude to science and metaphysics. Deserves careful study.

Swinburne, A. C. "Dethroning Tennyson," *Nineteenth Century*, XXIII (January-June, 1888), 127-129.

Swinburne, by pretending to prove that Darwin was the author of Tennyson's poems, pokes fun at the contenders that Bacon wrote Shakespeare's plays. The little essay shows Swinburne's wide knowledge of Tennyson's poems and emphasizes the scientific element in Tennyson's work.

Watkins, Watkin. *The Birds of Tennyson*. London: Porter, 1903.

Illustrated by G. E. Lodge. Collects and explains the many references to birds in the poems of Tennyson.

Watts, Theodore. "Aspects of Tennyson. 5. Tennyson as a Nature Poet," *Nineteenth Century*, XXXIII (May 1893), 836-856.

A careful study, one of a series of obituary articles by distinguished contemporaries probably commissioned by the editor, Tennyson's friend, Sir James Knowles.

6

Poems Not Included in the Collected Edition

Paden, W. D. "Twenty New Poems Attributed to Tennyson, Praed and Landor: Part One," *Victorian Studies*, IV (March 1961), 195-218.

In "Poems recovered from two literary journals edited by F. D. Maurice, 1828-29," the author attributed eleven poems to Tennyson. Mr. Paden gives an excellent and thoroughly documented account of the journals. The eleven poems attributed to Tennyson are "Hecatompylos," "Man's First Love," "To Julian," "Sonnet—The Boat," "Oh, Would I Were a Bird," "Dream of the West Wind," "The Statues," "Sweet Bird," "Sonnet—Where Is Now the Sunny Gleam," and "Sister, Sing the Song I Love."

Ricks, Christopher. "Tennyson's 'Rifle Clubs'," *Review of English Studies*, N.S., XV, No. 60 (November 1964), 401-4.

Prints a hitherto unpublished poem "Rifle Clubs" from a MS in Emily Tennyson's hand, corrected by the poet, now in the Baptist Library at Boston College, Massachusetts.

Ricks, Christopher. "Tennyson: Three Notes," *Modern Philology*, LXII, No. 2 (November 1964), 139-141.

Quotes (a) an omitted stanza from *Come Not, When I Am Dead*, (b) a note by F. T. Palgrave suggesting that Tennyson's description of the spouting fountain in "The Vision of Sin" was suggested by one of J. M. W. Turner's pictures, and (c) a poem "The Penny Wise," published by Tennyson in three periodicals in 1852.

Tennyson, Alfred Lord. "The Christ of Ammergau," *The Twentieth Century*, CLVII (January 1955), 2-3.

A poem extemporized by Tennyson to James Knowles in about 1870, after hearing that the man who played the part of Christ in the Passion Play had been carried off for military service. There is also a reference to the recent definition of the Pope's claim to infallibility. The poem was found among Knowles's papers by his granddaughter.

Tennyson, Alfred Lord. *The Devil and the Lady*, ed. with an introduction and notes by Sir Charles Tennyson. London and New York: Macmillan, 1930.

Blank verse play written by Tennyson in his 15th year. This and the early poems included in the volume just mentioned provide convincing evidence of his precocity and important material for studying the development of his art and thought. The contents of both volumes were issued with an introduction by Professor Rowland L. Collins in a single volume by the Indiana University Press in 1964.

Tennyson, Alfred. *Unpublished Early Poems*, ed. with an introduction and notes by Sir Charles Tennyson. London and New York: Macmillan, 1932.

An important record of the poet's adolescence.

Tennyson, Charles. "Tennyson's Unpublished Poems," *The Nineteenth Century*, CIX (March 1931), 367-380; (April 1931), 495-508; (May 1931), 625-636.

Presentation of "a number of unpublished poems and fragments by Tennyson . . . all from manuscripts left by him to his son Hallam, Lord Tennyson," who in turn left them to Sir Charles with power to publish. The bulk of the poems were afterwards included in *Unpublished Early Poems*.

Thomson, J. C., ed. *Suppressed Poems of Alfred, Lord Tennyson, 1830-1862*. New York: Harper Brothers, 1904.

Purports to give "with a few insignificant exceptions, all the poems at one time deemed by Tennyson worthy of publication, and afterwards rigorously suppressed." A short and rather depreciatory introduction. A useful volume for reference, but the reader should beware of misprints.

Thomson, J. C., ed. *The Suppressed Poems of Alfred, Lord Tennyson 1830-1868*. London: Sands and Co., 1910.

Contains 158 pages of "poems written and published by Tennyson during his active literary career and ultimately rejected as unsatisfactory." A reprint by the same editor of the poems included in his volume of 1904 (see preceding item) with three small lyrics added, but without the depreciatory introduction.

7

Annotated Editions and Selections

Auden, W. H. *Tennyson: an Introduction and a Selection.* London: Phoenix House, 1945.
    A very singular volume. The selection (266 pages) is an interesting one, and the introduction contains some stimulating passages, but the book is very carelessly produced. There are several elementary mistakes of fact, and one nine-line lyric is ruined by the, no doubt accidental, omission of the last three lines. The rather jaunty introduction contains many highly controversial statements, at least one of which has aroused universal condemnation.

Blunden, Edmund. *Selected Poems of Tennyson.* London: Heinemann, 1960.
    The introduction is worth attention as the work of a poet of distinction.

Boas, Guy. *Tennyson and Browning Contrasted.* New York: Nelson, 1925.
    A volume in the "Teaching of English" series, under the general editorship of Sir Henry Newbolt, containing 15 pages of introduction and 250 of selections.

Burton, Hester. *Tennyson. Selection and Commentary.* Oxford: Oxford University Press, 1954.
    197 pages of selections, including extracts from some of the longer poems, interspersed with a running commentary, biographical, technical, and expository. The author aims at giving the reader a selection showing not only the high quality of Tennyson's best work, but also the wide range of subject matter, style, and mood.

De Vane, William Clyde, and Mabel Phillips De Vane. *Selections from Tennyson.* New York: Crofts, 1940.
    Introduction, annotations, bibliography, poems arranged according to dates of publication. A full selection with useful notes. Introduction still somewhat influenced by the reaction.

Gawsworth, John. *Poetical Works of Tennyson.* Selected, with an Introduction. London: Macdonald, 1951.

About 430 pages of selections, no extracts. 15 pages of introduction. "Tennyson selected is indeed Tennyson resurrected."

Houghton, Walter E. and G. Robert Stange. *Victorian Poetry and Poetics.* Boston: Houghton Mifflin Company, 1959.

Contains a generous selection of Tennyson's poetry. The general introduction and the introduction of the Tennyson selection are worth study.

Huxley, Aldous. *Texts and Pretexts. An Anthology With Commentaries.* London: Chatto and Windus, 1932.

The few references to Tennyson are worth consideration only to the anthologist.

Jagger, Hubert. *Selections from Tennyson.* London: J. M. Dent and Sons, 1921.

About 190 pages (small octavo) of selections, with short introduction, a short life of Tennyson, a commentary on Tennyson's methods of versification, and some exercises for students.

Meynell, Alice Christiana. *Poems by Alfred, Lord Tennyson,* with an Introduction. Red Letter Library. London: Blackie and Son, 1904.

Less than three pages of introduction, but noteworthy as expressing the views of a distinguished poetess.

Mulliner, Beatrice C. *Tennyson's Shorter Poems and Lyrics,* ed. with introduction and notes. *Tennyson's English Idylls and Other Poems, 1842-1855,* ed. with introduction and notes. Oxford: Oxford University Press, 1909.

In the second volume the poems are arranged and considered under classified headings. The books are primarily for schools, but the notes have some value.

Rolfe, W. J. *Tennyson's Poetical Works.* "Cambridge Edition." Boston and New York: Houghton Mifflin Company, 1898.

Includes the poems up to and including Tennyson's volume of 1889, and the plays. An appendix includes the poems in *Poems by Two Brothers* attributed to Alfred Tennyson, and a number of suppressed poems and passages. There is a full and often useful appendix of "Notes and Illustrations."

Southam, B. C. *Selected Poems of Lord Tennyson.* Edited with introduction and notes. London: Chatto and Windus, 1964.

Though compiled primarily for schools, the volume is worth study for the novelty of its approach and appreciation.

Squire, Sir John. *Selected Poems of Tennyson.* London: Macmillan, 1947.

285 pages of selections and extracts with 12 pages of introduction, which concludes, "an abiding love of Tennyson I will allow no one to deny me." The introduction contains a delightful story of Tennyson told to Squire by Sir E. Gosse.

Stubbs, John Heath. *Poems of Alfred, Lord Tennyson.* London: Grey Walls Press, 1949.

A very brief selection of poems and extracts aimed at representing "the essential, personal and individual Tennyson," the selector considering Tennyson's "official poetry" (including the greater part of his sentimental narratives and would-be philosophic pieces) "dead to us today."

Tennyson, Sir Charles. *The Idylls of the King* and *The Princess,* London: Collins, 1956.

Short biographical introduction, chronological table, substantial introductions to *The Idylls of the King* and to *The Princess,* an analysis of Tennyson's blank verse, chronology of works, and bibliography.

Tennyson, Sir Charles. *Poems of Alfred, Lord Tennyson.* London: Collins, 1954.

A full selection of complete poems including the whole of *In Memoriam* and *Maud* (no extracts) with biographical introduction, bibliography, and notes.

Tennyson, Hallam Lord. *The Works of Tennyson Annotated.* The "Eversley Edition" in nine volumes. London and New York: Macmillan, 1907-1908.

Notes similar to the succeeding volume, but with the addition of substantial appendices, e.g. to the notes on *the Princess, Maud, In Memoriam, Idylls of the King,* and some of the dramas.

Tennyson, Hallam Lord. *The Works of Tennyson with Notes by the Author.* Edited with a Memoir by Hallam, Lord Tennyson. London: Macmillan, 1913.

The standard text. The notes have especial value, many of them having been dictated or approved by the poet.

Van Dyke, Henry. *Poems of Tennyson.* Selected with an introduction. New York: Scribners, 1920.

The introduction is in six parts, dealing with Tennyson's place in the 19th century; an outline of his life; his use of his sources; his revision of his text; the classification of his poems; and the qualities of his poetry. It is carefully written and with understanding, and can be read with profit.

Sources

Collins, John Churton. *Illustrations of Tennyson*. London: Chatto and Windus, 1891.
    An enquiry by one of the strongest of the Victorian critics into the nature and extent of Tennyson's "indebtedness to the poets who have preceded him." A very valuable study though some of the parallels suggested are very unconvincing. Based on three articles published in the *Cornhill Magazine* in 1880 and 1881.

Ford, George H. *Keats and the Victorians*. New Haven: Yale University Press, 1944.
    Part one, "Tennyson," contains an interesting discussion of Tennyson's part in establishing Keats' reputation and Tennyson's debt to Keats' influence.

Lester, George. *Lord Tennyson and the Bible*. London: Howe and Co., n.d.
    Four hundred and fifty Biblical allusions and parallelisms in Tennyson's work. Page numbers of quotations are from the 1889 Macmillan edition of the *Works* and the 1889 *Demeter* volume.

Loane, George Green. *Echoes in Tennyson, and Other Essays*. London: Stockwell, 1928.
    Adds a few specimens to those already noted in Churton Collins's *Illustrations of Tennyson*.

Mcldrum, Elizabeth. "Tennyson and the Classical Poets," *Contemporary Review*, CLXXV, No. 100 (May 1949), 296-299.
    A brief but useful study. Contrasts the influence of Classical authors on Shelley, Milton, and Tennyson, and analyzes Tennyson's classical references in some detail. Concludes that these authors must have had a good influence on Tennyson with his love of word-music, which, she considers, tends to excess and meaninglessness, and sentimentality.

Mustard, Wilfrid Pirt. *Classical Echoes in Tennyson.* New York: Macmillan, 1904.

Tennyson was a constant student of the Greek and Roman classics, abundant evidence being found in his poetry. Mustard begins with the influence of Homer and goes on through the Greeks and Latins to St. Augustine.

Paden, W. D. "MT. 1352: Jacques de Vitry, The Mensa Philosophica, Hödeken, and Tennyson," *Journal of American Folklore,* LVIII (January 1945), 35-47.

Traces the source of Tennyson's youthful play, *The Devil and the Lady,* to an article by Francis Cohen (later Sir Francis Palgrave) on "Popular Mythology of the Middle Ages," in the *Quarterly Review* for January 1820.

Paden, W. D. "Tennyson and Persian Poetry Again," *Modern Language Notes,* LVIII (December 1943), 652-656.

Strongly criticizes the views of J. D. Yohannan. A reply by Yohannan is appended on p. 656.

Paden, W. D. "Tennyson and Persian Poetry Once More," *Modern Language Notes,* LX (April 1945), 284.

Disposes of the theory that Tennyson had been led to model a lyric in *The Princess* on the Persian Ghazal because of information received from Fitzgerald's friend Cowell. See also *Tennyson and the Princess* by John Killham, Chapter X.

Potwin, L. S. "The Source of Tennyson's 'The Lady of Shalott'," *Modern Language Notes,* XVII (December 1902), 473-477.

Suggests that one source used by Tennyson was No. LXXXI in the collection of *novellas* printed in Milan in 1804 and referred to by John Churton Collins in his *Early Poems of Alfred, Lord Tennyson.* Potwin points out that the novella only really resembles Tennyson's poem in the description of the funeral journey.

Robinson, Edna Moore. *Tennyson's Use of the Bible.* Baltimore: Johns Hopkins Press, 1917.

Orderly presentation of Tennyson's references to scripture (1) according to their appearance in the Bible, and (2) according to the final published order of Tennyson's poems.

Van Dyke, Henry. "The Bible in Tennyson," *The Century* (August 1889), 515-532.

A brief study not without value.

Warren, T. Herbert. "Tennyson and Dante," *Monthly Review*, XIV (January 1904), 117-138.

A useful summary by the President of Magdalen College, Oxford, of the more obvious references. Not a study in depth.

Yohannan, J. D. "Tennyson and Persian Poetry," *Modern Language Notes*, LVII (February 1942), 83-92.

Suggests that the effect of Tennyson's reading of Persian poetry with Edward Fitzgerald and E. B. Cowell and in Sir William Jones's translations can be traced in certain of his poems. See also under W. D. Paden above.

9

Bibliographies, Concordances, Handbooks

Arnold, William Harris. "My Tennyson," *Scribner's Magazine*, LXXI (May 1922), 589-601.
    Of bibliographical interest. Describes important Tennyson items in the author's collection.

Baker, Arthur Ernest. *A Concordance to "The Devil and the Lady."* London: Golden Vista Press, 1931.

Baker, Arthur Ernest. *A Concordance to the Poetical and Dramatic Works of Alfred, Lord Tennyson.* London: Kegan Paul, Trench, Trubner, 1914.
    The Baker concordances are standard.

Baker, Arthur Ernest. *A Tennyson Dictionary.* London: Routledge, 1916.
    Characters and place-names contained in the poetical and dramatic works of the poet, alphabetically arranged and described; synopses of the poems and plays.

Bateson, F. W., ed. *Cambridge Bibliography of English Literature.* Cambridge: Cambridge University Press, 1940. *Supplement*, Vol. V., 1957. "Tennyson," pp. 583-586.
    Aims at complete bibliography of the poems, whether collected, separately published, or in selections, and at a complete reference to critical material of importance. Biographical references less comprehensive. Foreign language items included. Tennyson occupies pp. 253-258 of Vol. III.

Baum, Paull Franklin. "Alfred, Lord Tennyson," in *The Victorian Poets, a Guide to Research*, ed. Frederick E. Faverty. Cambridge: Harvard University Press, 1956.
    Scholarly bibliography; emphasis on recent publications. Essay type presentation.

Collins, John Churton, ed. *The Early Poems of Alfred, Lord Tennyson*. London: Methuen, 1900.
 Introduction, various readings, and bibliography. After a valuable general introduction Collins, one of the leading critics of the late Victorian era, prints the text of the two volumes of 1842 with useful and scholarly notes. An appendix contains the poems originally included in the volumes of 1830 and 1833, distinguishing those which were afterwards republished, at different times, in the collected works, and those which were afterwards suppressed altogether.

Collins, John Churton, ed. *In Memoriam, The Princess*, and *Maud*. London: Methuen, 1902.
 With critical introduction, commentaries, and notes together with various readings. A valuable sequel to the volume mentioned above.

Dixon, William Macneile. *A Primer of Tennyson*. London: Methuen, 1896. Third edition, 1908.
 A useful introduction to the study of Tennyson. Bibliography, as far as it goes, is very good.

Ehrsam, T. G., R. H. Deily, and R. M. Smith. *Bibliographies of Twelve Victorian Authors*. New York: The H. W. Wilson Company, 1936.
 Includes published critical material in English and in foreign languages employing the Latin alphabet, also unpublished Masters' essays and Doctoral dissertations. Articles in daily newspapers not included. Closing date, end of 1934. The Tennyson bibliography occupies pp. 300-362.

Hughes, A. M. D. *Tennyson, Poems Published in 1842*. Oxford: Clarendon Press, 1914.
 A thirty-two page sketch of Tennyson's life, excellent notes, and variant readings from the texts of 1830 and 1832.

Luce, Morton. *A Handbook to the Works of Alfred, Lord Tennyson*. London: George Bell, 1908. First edition, 1895.
 Over 450 pages octavo. Written while Tennyson's fame was still near its peak. It is mostly interpretative or expository. May be of use for occasional reference.

L. S. L. [Livingston, Luther Samuel]. *Bibliography of the First Editions in Book Form of the Works of Alfred, Lord Tennyson*. New York: Dodd, Mead, 1901.

A chronological bibliography with descriptive and explanatory notes, issued before Thomas J. Wise's two volume, privately printed, bibliography, but with some knowledge of its contents.

Marshall, George O., Jr. *A Tennyson Handbook.* New York: Twayne Publishers, 1963.

Deals one by one with every poem and play ever in-included by Tennyson in a volume (even though afterwards suppressed by him) with bibliographical, biographical, and other relative information. Something is said of the contemporary reception of the poems and subsequent criticism. The author also frequently expresses his opinions. These are necessarily very briefly stated, often so briefly as to have little value, e.g., on *Idylls of the King,* 1859: "Tennyson's greatest claim to fame in his own day has been to succeeding generations his most distasteful work." As a factual record the book should be of great value to students.

Paden, W. D. "Note on the Variants of *In Memoriam* and *Lucretius*," *The Library,* Fifth series, VIII (1953), 269-273.

A valuable account of the text of Tennyson's *Lucretius.* Also see under Ricks, Christopher.

Quaritch, Bernard. *Description of an Important Collection of Holograph Manuscript Poems by Lord Tennyson in the Possession of Bernard Quaritch, and the Holograph Manuscript of "Sardanapalus" by Lord Byron.* London: 11 Grafton Street, 1914.

Ratchford, Fannie E. *An Exhibition of Manuscripts and Printed Books at the University of Texas, October 1-30, 1942, Alfred, Lord Tennyson, 1809-1892.* Austin: University of Texas Press, 1942.

Value for the student lies in the description of the Tennyson material collected by John Henry Wrenn and knowledge of its location.

Ricks, Christopher. "Tennyson's 'Lucretius'," *The Library* (March 1965), 63-64.

Mr. Ricks compares the text sent to *Macmillan's Magazine* in May 1868 (with an inserted letter addressed to Alexander Macmillan) with the published text. See also under Paden, W. D., above.

Shannon, Edgar F., Jr. "The History of a Poem: Tennyson's 'Ode on the Death of the Duke of Wellington'," *Studies in Bibliography, Papers of the Bibliographical Society of the University of Virginia*, XIII (1960), 149-177.
"An account of the composition, reception, and revision of the poem and an appendix of variorum readings illustrate Tennyson's scrupulous craftsmanship and his increasing willingness, as poet laureate, to speak affirmatively to the people."

Shannon, Edgar F., Jr. "Literary Manuscripts of Alfred Tennyson in the Harvard College Library," *Harvard Library Bulletin*, X, No. 2 (Spring 1956), 254-274.
Describes the most important collection of Tennyson MSS in the world. A claim might no doubt be made for the collection of MSS at Trinity College, Cambridge, but this is not available for use by scholars.

Shannon, Edgar F., Jr. "Lord Tennyson," *Victorian Newsletter* (Autumn 1957), 26-27.
A brief survey of the principal deposits of Tennyson materials in the U. S. A. and Great Britain, compiled before the establishment of the Tennyson Room and Tennyson Research Centre at Lincoln, England.

Shannon, Edgar F., Jr. "The Proof of *Gareth and Lynette* in the Widener Collection," *Papers of the Bibliographical Society of America*, XLI (1947), 321-340.

Shepherd, Richard Herne. *Tennysoniana*. London: Pickering and Co., 1879. Second edition. Revised and enlarged. Notes bibliographical and critical on early poems of Alfred and Charles Tennyson. Opinions of contemporary writers. *In Memoriam*; comparison with Shakespeare's sonnets; various readings. Various readings in later poems. Allusions to scripture and classical authors. The Tennyson portraits. Bibliographical list of Tennyson's volumes and his contributions to periodical publications, 1866-1875; 1879 revised and enlarged. Published anonymously, 1896.

[Shepherd, Richard Herne.] *The Bibliography of Tennyson*. London: printed for subscribers only, 1896.
Covers Tennyson's published and privately printed writings 1827-1896 inclusive. Compiled by a very conscientious and learned bibliographer. The very full notes still have value.

Tennyson, Sir Charles. *Tennyson Collection, Usher Gallery, Lincoln* (England). Catalogue with Foreword and annotations by Sir Charles Tennyson. City of Lincoln, Libraries, Museum and Art Gallery Committee, 1963.

A complete catalogue of this extremely important and comprehensive collection of about 400 items, with very full annotations. This does not include the very important mass of material in the Tennyson Research Centre at Lincoln which is not yet catalogued.

Thomson, J. C. *Bibliography of the Writings of Alfred, Lord Tennyson.* Wimbledon: J. Thomson, 1905.

Only 20 copies printed, one in British Museum. Thomson claims to include several of the rare trail issues unknown to Herne Shepherd and to have received assistance from T. J. Wise.

Wise, Thomas J. *A Bibliography of the Writings of Alfred, Lord Tennyson.* 2 vols. London: Printed for Private Circulation, 1908. 100 copies printed.

Vol. I, Part I; a chronological bibliography of all primary sources, beginning with *Poems by Two Brothers*, 1827, and ending with *The Antechamber*, 1906. Vol. I, Part II, lists contributions to periodicals; Vol. II Part III, pirated issues; Part IV, collected editions; Part V, complete volumes of Biography and criticism; Part VI, alphabetical list. Reproductions of title pages, textual description, and analyses; historical accounts are given for each publication. The most nearly complete bibliography in existence.

10

Critical and Interpretative: General

Abercrombie, Lascelles. "Tennyson," *Revaluations: Studies in Biography*. London: Oxford University Press, 1931, pp. 60-76.
A distinguished poet attacks the reaction against Tennyson. Tennyson's life was wholly given to his art and his peculiar excellence will remain as long as man's delight in earth and human nature remains.

Austin, Alfred. "The Poetry of the Period," *Temple Bar*, XXVI (July 1869), 179-194. Reprinted in *The Poetry of the Period*. London: Bentley, 1870.
Tennyson's successor as Poet Laureate declares with "a confidence not the growth of yesterday, but of long, deliberate, and ever deepening convictions," that "Mr. Tennyson has no pretensions to be called a great poet . . . not even at the head of the poets of the third rank, among which he must ultimately take his place." Compares Tennyson unfavourably with Byron, Shelley, and Wordsworth, without, however, much justifying criticism.

Austin, Alfred. "On a Recent Criticism of Mr. Swinburne's," *Macmillan's Magazine*, XLIII, No. 257 (March 1881), 399-408.
In this article the author recanted the harsh criticism of Tennyson contained in his *Poetry of the Period*. See also Austin's review of *Demeter and Other Poems* in the *National Review* (December 1889), 694-702.

Bagehot, Walter. "Wordsworth, Tennyson, and Browning," in *Literary Studies*, II. London: Longmans Green, 1905.
A brilliant and very influential study reviewing Tennyson's *Enoch Arden* and Browning's *Dramatis Personae*. Bagehot divides poetry into pure, ornate, and grotesque, and treats the three poets mentioned as exponents of the three types in the above order. Tennyson, he suggests, had written "pure" art in his Lincolnshire poems. He could have so described a real sailor had he wished, but deliberately chose the ornate form

because he was not concerned to present real people experiencing actual emotions. *Enoch Arden* has never recovered in critical estimation from this attack, though it remains one of Tennyson's most popular poems.

Ball, Patricia M. "Tennyson and the Romantics," *Victorian Poetry*, I (January 1963), 7-16.

Considers and usefully extends the analysis of Langbaum in his *The Poetry of Experience*.

Basler, Roy P. "Tennyson the Psychologist," *South Atlantic Quarterly*, XLIII (April 1944), 143-159. Reprinted in Basler, Roy P. *Sex, Symbolism and Psychology in Literature*. New Brunswick: Rutgers University Press, 1948.

A study of *Maud*, which, the author maintains, antedates the writings of Sigmund Freud by half a century and anticipates the complex "Constructive" method of Jung. A very valuable study of an almost untouched but extremely important subject. The author may be thought now and then to read rather too much into Tennyson's statements.

Bateson, Frederick W. *Romantic Schizophrenia. English Poetry, a Critical Introduction*. New York: Longmans, 1950.

Bateson sets up the theme of the Victorian split personality, saying it is in a sense the reflection of the split in Victorian society. In Chapter XII, 223-233, "Tears, Idle Tears" is presented as romantic schizophrenia, the social conflict in Tennyson being between his conscience and his imagination. The "days that are no more" are both the historic past and the unhappy twenties.

Baum, Paull Franklin. *Tennyson Sixty Years After*. Chapel Hill: University of North Carolina Press, 1948.

A critical study with aesthetic approach; denies Tennyson intellectual depth; belongs to the reaction movement in spite of its date.

Bayne, Peter. *Lessons from My Masters, Carlyle, Tennyson and Ruskin*. London: James Clark and Co., 1879.

Worth a glance as a typical example of the almost entirely eulogistic study of a mid-Victorian admirer. Pp. 195-332 relate to Tennyson.

Benziger, James. *Images of Eternity*. Carbondale: Southern Illinois University Press, 1962.

These "Studies in the Poetry of Religious Vision," from

Wordsworth to T. S. Eliot, include a long essay on Tennyson (pp. 138-189). In this the author dwells on certain inherent weaknesses which he claims to perceive in the poet's character and intellect, and their effect on his poetry. He concludes, however, that Tennyson must not be judged by his weaknesses only.

Berry, Francis. *Poetry and the Physical Voice*. London: Routledge and Kegan Paul, 1962.

After two very concentrated chapters on "Problems of Hearing and Saying," and "The Voice in Time," the author tries "to bring into awareness three individual physical voices, which we ought to hear behind—or through—the poetical works of Tennyson, Shelley and Milton." He comes to the conclusion that Tennyson composed in terms of his own voice and was a prisoner of that voice, however capacious the dimensions of that prison. An original and highly suggestive work much of which is, necessarily, very controversial.

Bowden, Marjorie Moreland (Sansom). *Tennyson in France*. Manchester: Manchester University Press, 1930.

A study of French critical opinion. Traces the history of Tennyson in France from a purely literary point of view, shows the extent to which he gained appreciation, and the part he played in influencing the French poetic outlook towards the end of the century.

Bradley, A[ndrew] C[ecil]. *Oxford Lectures on Poetry*. London: Macmillan, 1909.

The Long Poem in the Age of Wordsworth," pp. 177-208 contains on pp. 192-193 a well-considered criticism of the *Idylls of the King:*

"In spite of countless beauties, the total result was disappointing, not merely from the defects of this or that poem, but because the old unity of spirit and story was broken up, and the new was neither equal to the old nor complete in itself."

In a footnote Bradley deprecates the prevalent depreciation of Tennyson's genius. "I admire and love his poetry with all my heart, and regard him as considerably our greatest poet since Wordsworth."

Bradley, Andrew Cecil. "The Reaction Against Tennyson," *A Miscellany*. London: Macmillan, 1929. Also in *English Association Pamphlets*, XXXIX. Oxford University Press, 1917.

A strong and intelligent attack on "The Reaction against Tennyson."

Brimley, George. "Alfred Tennyson's Poems," *Cambridge Essays.* London: John W. Parker, 1855, pp. 226-281.

Deals with the poems up till and including *Maud.* Finds Tennyson "possessing the clearest insight into our modern life . . . what Shakespeare and Chaucer did for the ages they lived in, Tennyson is doing for our age, after his measure."

Brooke, Stopford Augustus. "Tennyson," *Contemporary Review,* LXII (July-December, 1892), 761-785.

A full and useful survey, emphasizes Tennyson's essential simplicity and his high estimate of the poet's function; and discusses his attitude towards Christianity, patriotism, human freedom, sociology, progress, and other such questions.

Brooke, Stopford Augustus. *Tennyson, His Art and Relation to Modern Life.* New York: G. P. Putnam's Sons, 1894. London: Isbister and Company, 1894.

A bit outmoded, but still has value.

Browning, Elizabeth Barrett. *Alfred Tennyson: Notes and Comments.* London: Printed for private circulation only by Richard Clay and Sons Ltd., 1919.

Two short letters to R. H. Horne, dated December 16, 1843, and July 20, 1844. The first classes Tennyson with Wordsworth and Keats. The second is mainly devoted to a defence of E. B. B.'s rhyme schemes.

Browning, Robert. *An Opinion of the Writings of Alfred, Lord Tennyson.* With a statement of his changed views regarding Percy Bysshe Shelley. London: Printed for private circulation only by Richard Clay and Sons, 1920.

With no commentary other than the title, the book consists of five letters from Robert Browning, four being to Isa Blagden, dated Nov. 30, 1859; June 19, 1862; Feb. 19, 1867; Jan. 19, 1870. One letter to Buxton Forman, dated Dec. 27, 1877. The letter dated January 19th, 1870, to Isa Blagden contains the critical statements. Browning's attitude is very adverse towards Tennyson's new book, *The Holy Grail and Other Poems.*

Buchanan, Robert. "Tennyson's Charm," *Saint Paul's Magazine,* X (March 1872), 282-303.

This article, extremely high in its praise of Tennyson, is balanced by overtones which suggest the direction taken by later critics.

Buckley, Jerome Hamilton. *Poems of Tennyson*. Selected with an Introduction and Notes. Cambridge: The Riverside Press, 1958.

525 pages of selections from the whole range of Tennyson's poetry, including the whole of *In Memoriam* and seven of the *Idylls of the King*. In his important twelve page introduction Professor Buckley states that his purpose has been to suggest not only Tennyson's power but also the course of his growth as an artist, and that his selection, while attempting to illustrate the poet's entire thematic range, lays particular and rather uncommon stress on the poems which examine the nature of poetry and the role of the poet.

Buckley, Jerome Hamilton. *Tennyson: The Growth of a Poet*. Cambridge: Harvard University Press, 1960.

Professor Buckley aims in this book at studying Tennyson's developing sensibility as a guide to a critical evaluation of his accomplishment, while making it clear that each poem must be detached once again from its source in the imaginative life of the poet to be judged in terms of its own intrinsic qualities as a poetic unit. Professor Buckley has had the advantage of access to the great mass of MSS and other Tennyson material recently acquired by Harvard University, where he is Professor of Victorian Literature. His study is careful and comprehensive and his views always balanced and well considered.

Bush, Douglas. *Mythology and the Romantic Tradition in English Poetry*. Cambridge: Harvard University Press, 1937.

"Tennyson," Chapter VI, pp. 197-228, is the standard treatment of Tennyson's classical poems.

Bush, Douglas. "The Personal Note in Tennyson's Classical Poems," *University of Toronto Quarterly*, IV (January 1935), 201-218.

This material was used later in *Mythology and the Romantic Tradition*.

Carr, Arthur J. "Tennyson as a Modern Poet," *University of Toronto Quarterly*, XIX (1950), 361-382. In John Killham, *Critical Essays*, pp. 41-64.

A careful and thorough analysis of Tennyson's poetic progress, leading to some interesting if controversial conclusions. "The price that Tennyson pays for being a representative poet is great. He suffers our disease and our confusion. . . . It is a vicarious role, and we heap on him our detested sins . . . he kept to the midstream of his culture. As a result he works out remorselessly the fatal consequences of our romantic tradition. . . . After him the deluge, the spreading chaos of modern art. He is one of its makers."

Chesterton, G. K. *The Uses of Diversity*. London: The Library Press, 1925.

The chapter, "Tennyson," pp. 18-23, expresses astonishment at the critical depreciation of Tennyson. But admits that he was a "partial failure"—chiefly because he was the poet of popular science. "His feet were set on things transitory and untenable, compromises and compacts of silence. Yet he was so perfect a poet that I fancy he will still be able to stand, even upon such clouds."

Chesterton, G. K. *The Victorian Age in Literature*. London: Williams and Norgate, 1913.

Chapters I, "The Victorian Compromise," and III, "The Great Victorian Poets," are stimulating, provocative, and often really illuminating.

Cohen, J. M. "*In Memoriam:* A Hundred Years After," *Cornhill Magazine*, CLXIV (Autumn 1949), 151-164.

A long essay very much on the lines of Harold Nicolson. The author finds the emotion in Tennyson's poems before *In Memoriam* "monotonous and dilute." After *In Memoriam* he is a great figure but seldom a good poet. . . . Only into *In Memoriam* did all his virtues flow."

Collins, John Churton. "Tennyson," *Posthumous Essays*. London: J. M. Dent, 1912, pp. 242-255.

A brief survey by a distinguished critic, probably composed as a lecture soon after Tennyson's death. It concludes, "It may be—but that posterity will decide—that what appeals to our day, to us as a nation, preponderates over what is of permanent and universal interest . . . and that in the Valhalla of the future he will not take his place among the classics of the human race. Still of one thing we may be sure, that no name will ever be more loved and honoured in that island and by that race . . . for which he so nobly wrought."

Danzig, Allan. "The Contraries: a Central Concept in Tennyson's Poetry," *PMLA*, LXXVII (December 1962), 577-585.

Being a thinker, Tennyson was always concerned with contrary relationships: in the sensual world, in human affairs, in abstract thought. Mr. Danzig presents an excellent treatment of Tennyson's dualistic universe.

Dawson, W. J. *Makers of Modern Poetry.* London: Hodder and Stoughton, 1899.

Pages 169-269 are devoted to Tennyson. "That he is among the few great creative poets of humanity, no one will assert; that he is nevertheless a poet of great and varied excellence, none will deny . . . while in Tennyson artistic culture has never been surpassed, yet the original poetic impulse is weaker in him than in Wordsworth and Milton." A full and careful study.

De la Mare, Walter. *Pleasures and Speculations.* London: Faber and Faber, 1940.

Contains an essay on Tennyson by one of the most distinguished of his poetic successors: from *Times Literary Supplement.*

Devey, J. *A Comparative Estimate of Modern English Poets.* London: Moxon, 1873.

Chapter XI, "The Art School," contains an elaborate criticism of Tennyson's poetic method. "His poetry, like that of the architectural fashions and dogmatic views of the day, seems to be the result of a capricious eclecticism. . . . But considering his contracted standpoint, Tennyson has perhaps achieved as much as could be achieved by a poet in his situation."

Dixon, William Macneile. *A Primer of Tennyson with a Critical Essay.* London: Methuen, 1896.

Denies Tennyson the highest imagination but admits that "there is no body of English verse, wherein for eye, ear and heart a feast of purer, more unalloyed pleasure is spread." Though aware of the deeper levels of Tennyson's poetry, Dixon perhaps does not give them enough weight, but his survey is sympathetic and scholarly.

D. J. G. [Donald J. Gray]. *Review of Critical Essays on the Poetry of Tennyson,* ed. John Killham; and *Tennyson* by Jerome H. Buckley, *Victorian Studies,* IV, No. 3 (March 1961), 274-276.

A valuable survey of contemporary criticism.

Donahue, Mary Joan. "Tennyson's 'Hail Briton!' and 'Tithon' in the Heath Manuscript," *PMLA*, LXIV (June 1949), 385-416.

Deals with an early poem in the *In Memoriam* metre, which Tennyson never published, but many stanzas and lines of which were used by him in later publications. Valuable insight on Tennyson's methods of composition.

Dowden, Edward. "Mr. Tennyson and Mr. Browning," *The Afternoon Lectures on Literature and Art*. London: Bell and Daldy, 1869.

Compares the views of the two poets in regard to such subjects as Law, Progress, Love. An interesting study, which, however, was written before either poet had reached the final stage of his development. Also London: Kegan Paul, 1878.

Drinkwater, John. "Victorian Poets," *Outline of Literature*. London: George Newnes, 1923, pp. 425-434.

An interesting survey by a distinguished poet, published in the same year as Nicolson's *Tennyson*. Finds that Tennyson excels in vividness of drawing and variety of subject and holds the highest place among the followers of Keats, but that he has no pretence to match the mighty scale of *Hyperion* and wants the "deep poetic charm" which marks Keats's finest work.

Duncan, Edgar Hill. "Tennyson: A Modern Appraisal," *Tennessee Studies in Literature*, IV (1959), 13-30.

Begins with a summary of the generally accepted appraisal of Tennyson as laid down in 1917 by Grierson. Duncan then joins the opposition to the reaction against Tennyson by making an excellent analysis of *Ulysses*. An excellent survey of 20th century criticism.

Eliot, T. S. "In Memoriam," *Essays Ancient and Modern*. London: Faber and Faber, 1936. *Critical Essays*, ed. John Killham, pp. 207-215.

This essay is the most influential piece of Tennyson criticism published since Harold Nicholson's *Tennyson*. It opens with a comprehensive statement of Tennyson's claim to greatness. "Tennyson is a great poet for reasons that are perfectly clear. He has three qualities which are seldom found together except in the greatest poets: abundance, variety, and complete technical competence." The essay contains much profound criticism and some highly controversial statements. It deserves careful consideration by all Tennyson students.

Elton, Oliver. *Alfred Tennyson and Matthew Arnold.* London: Edward Arnold and Co., 1924.
    Two essays from Elton's *Survey of English Literature, 1830-1880,* published 1920. Between the *Inaugural Lecture,* 1901, and *The Survey,* 1920, the author moved to a more favorable attitude towards Tennyson. The essay on Tennyson, pp. 1-54, is a logical grouping of the most important poems within a chronological frame, giving a rapid evaluation of content and technique.

Elton, Oliver. "Tennyson: an Inaugural Lecture," *Modern Studies.* London: Edward Arnold, 1907. (Lecture, 1901; reprinted, 1907.)
    An able essay of the reaction. Elton credits Tennyson with "a temper and intellect of large design . . . a curious, a noble, and a various invention in metre . . . a mastery of the sensuous image" and of "the representation of difficult and shadowy feelings," but he considers it an illusion to think of him as "a great remedial thinker," and maintains that he "leaves no great imaginative whole," and that "his ruling conceptions are vanishing into a past of shadows."

Fairchild, Hoxie N. " 'Wild Bells' in Bailey's *Festus?*" *Modern Language Notes,* LXIV (April 1949), 256-258.
    A comparison of Festus's prayer in P. J. Bailey's *Festus,* 1839, and *In Memoriam,* section CVI.

Fausset, Hugh I'Anson. *Tennyson: A Modern Portrait.* New York: Appleton, 1923.
    Fausset was overshadowed by Harold Nicolson in the reaction against Tennyson. The *Modern Portrait* seems to be a post-war drama in which Fausset, the embittered antagonist, attacks his own idea of Victorian England, here personified as Alfred, Lord Tennyson, the protagonist.

Fausset, Hugh I'Anson. *Poets and Pundits: a Collection of Essays.* New Haven: Yale University Press, 1947.
    "The Hidden Tennyson," pp. 187-191, is a discerning treatment of the poet and the climate of opinion in which he worked. Both style and content denote increased maturity since Fausset's 1923 *Tennyson.*

Fox, W. J. *Lectures Addressed Chiefly to the Working Classes.* London: Charles Fox, 1845.
    Lecture 15, which deals with Tennyson, is interesting as showing the views of a sympathetic contemporary radical, conscious of a divergence of political creed.

Garnet, Richard and Gilbert Keith Chesterton. *Tennyson*. London: Hodder and Stoughton, 1908.
 An essay showing Tennyson's relation to his age, with emphasis on ideas.

Gingerich, Solomon Francis. *Wordsworth, Tennyson and Browning. A Study in Human Freedom*. Ann Arbor, Michigan: George Wahr, 1911.
 A dissertation, University of Michigan, 1909. In the 1911 edition, Tennyson is discussed on pp. 113-175. Treats the mystical and transcendental experience of spiritual freedom, including such topics as memory and the mystic element, freedom and law, art and law, with stress on the power of will as the root of human personality.

Gissing, George Robert. *Autobiographical and Imaginative Selections*. Biographical and critical notes by his son, A. C. Gissing. London: Jonathan Cape, 1928.
 Comments of an eminent novelist on Tennyson, Huxley, and others.

[Gladstone, William Ewart.] "Idylls of the King," *Quarterly Review*, CVI (October 1859), 454-485. Reprinted in *Gleanings of Past Years*, II, pp. 131-177. London: John Murray, 1879, and in *Famous Reviews*, p. 12., ed. B. Johnson. London, New York, and Melbourne: Pitman, 1914.
 This long review by one of the greatest and most representative of Victorians deserves careful study. It contains a valuable estimate of the stature of Arthur Hallam, who was the author's close friend. The review emphasizes the transcendent merits of *In Memoriam* and the *Idylls of the King*, of 1859, in which year the original review was composed. The reaction to *Maud* is much less favourable, largely because of the apparently warlike tendency of Part III. A note written by Gladstone in 1879 largely recants this view.

"A Great National Poet: Tennyson's Mystic Imperialism," *Times Literary Supplement*, October 10, 1942, p. 498.
 Article celebrating the 50th anniversary of Tennyson's death. It should be compared with the *Times Literary Supplement* article of Aug. 5, 1909. Stresses the cosmic elements in Tennyson's poetry and dwells on those features of his work which were unnoticed by the 1909 article. On the opposite page is a leading article emphasizing the points taken in the first article.

Grierson, Herbert J. C. "The Tennysons," *The Cambridge History of English Literature*, ed. A. W. Ward and A. R. Waller, XIII, pp. 25-53. Cambridge: Cambridge University Press, 1916. (New Impression, 1922).

Written with great strength and clarity, stressing the delineation of mood as Tennyson's dominant characteristic, and preoccupation with the mysteries of life and death as the deepest vein of his poetic personality. Criticism of Tennyson since 1917 has been continuously and deeply influenced by Grierson's essay.

Groom, Bernard. "On the Diction of Tennyson, Browning, and Arnold," *Society for Pure English*. Tract No. 53. Oxford: Clarendon Press, 1939. Reprinted in *The Diction of Poetry from Spenser to Bridges*. Toronto: University of Toronto Press, 1955.

A valuable study on the choice and use of words by the poets named. An attempt is also made to relate the diction of each poet to the quality of his work.

Gwynn, Stephen. *Tennyson: A Critical Study*. London: Blackie and Sons, 1899.

Intelligent criticism covering a wide area. Interesting as coming at the very end of Tennyson's period of great popularity.

Hallam, Arthur Henry. "On Some Characteristics of Modern Poetry and on the Lyrical Poems of Alfred Tennyson," *Englishman's Magazine*, I (August 1831), 616-628. Reprinted in *The Writings of Arthur Hallam*, ed. T. H. Vail Motter. New York: MLA of America, 1943. London: Oxford University Press, 1943.

This review was of crucial importance to Tennyson's career and poetic development and deserves the closest study.

Harrison, Frederic. *Tennyson, Ruskin, Mill, and Other Literary Estimates*. London: Macmillan, 1899.

A sincere and detailed study by an eminent Victorian man of letters and leading Positivist, who appreciates to the full Tennyson's mastery of form but finds his philosophic basis unsympathetic, and is not always able to appreciate his innovations and inner meaning. The essay concludes, "If we cannot claim for Tennyson the supreme place of a poet of man's destinies, or as one of the creative masters of our literature, he has forever clothed the softer aspects of the world of man and nature with a garment of delicate fancy and pure light."

Hearn, Lafcadio. *Appreciations of Poetry*. London: Heinemann, 1916. New York: Dodd, Mead and Co., 1916.

From lectures delivered by Hearn in Japan between 1896 and 1902. Chapter II, "Studies in Tennyson (a fragment)," is well worth reading though only six pages long and written in a simplified style for Japanese students. Concludes that Tennyson is not a world poet because of his deficiency in passion, but that "as an English poet, as a master of all the beauties and riches and powers of the English language, he is unique."

Henley, W. E. "Tennyson," in *Views and Reviews*. London: David Nutt, 1892.

This distinguished late Victorian poet and critic (1849-1903) finds Tennyson's later verse more "plangent and affecting," with a "larger and more liberal mastery of form," and a "finer, stronger, saner, sentiment of material" than in the "well filled times of *In Memoriam* and the Arthurian *Idylls*."

Horne, R. H., ed. *A New Spirit of the Age*. London: Smith, Elder and Co., 1844.

The chapter on Tennyson, pp. 2-32, considers the poet under four aspects: as a poet of fairy-land and enchantment; as a poet of profound sentiment in the affections; as a painter of pastoral nature; and as the delineator and representer of tragic emotions.

Houghton, Walter E. *The Victorian Frame of Mind, 1830-1870*. New Haven: Yale University Press, 1957.

A very full exploration of "the general ideas and attitudes about life which Victorians of the middle and upper classes would have breathed in with the air . . . the frame of mind in which they were living and thinking." A valuable book for background study.

House, Humphrey. "Tennyson," *All in Due Time*. London: Rupert Hart-Davis, 1955, pp. 121-129.

In this essay House finds Tennyson's thought "governed by the Time process and the evolutionary idea which accompanied it" and attributes to this influence his emphasis on action and on the description of external things.

Hutton, R. H. *Contemporary Thought and Thinkers*. London: Macmillan, 1894.

Volume II contains interesting comments on *Despair* and *Locksley Hall Sixty Years After* (Chapters XVIII and XIX).

James, David G. "Wordsworth and Tennyson," *Proceedings of the British Academy*, XXXVI (1950), 113-129. (Warton Lecture on English Poetry.)

An excellent and well reasoned comparison based chiefly on a study of *The Prelude* and *In Memoriam*, both of which were published in 1850. Concludes that Wordsworth is a greater poet than Tennyson because in his poetry the criticism of life is "profounder and a richer ennoblement of life." Wordsworth came to an assurance of the spiritual nature of the universe through poetic apprehension of the natural world. Tennyson's apprehensions do not act as a revelation and he does not attain Wordsworth's assurance. The author has perhaps not entirely understood the spiritual relevance of Tennyson's symbolism and may be to some extent misled by differences of approach and technique. Tennyson frequently said that his spiritual beliefs were founded not on what he saw in nature but what he *felt* in his own heart.

James, Henry. "Tennyson's Drama," *Views and Reviews*. Boston: Ball Publishing Co., 1908.

Contains a valuable survey of Tennyson's poetic achievement. (See under: Dramas General—post.)

Jamieson, Paul F. "Tennyson and His Audience in 1832," *Philological Quarterly*, XXXI (October 1952), 407-413.

Discusses the advantage to and effect on Tennyson of having "The Apostles" as a *coterie* audience during his early years.

Jennings, James George. *An Essay on Metaphor in Poetry*. With an appendix on the use of metaphor in Tennyson's *In Memoriam*. London: Blackie and Son, 1915.

Jennings first gives what literary critics have said about metaphor; Aristotle, Quintilian, Longinus, and several moderns; then turns to the poets. His thesis is that metaphor, a double language, supplies scenes to complete and correct the partial nature of action or theme, and supplies a background, ever shifting, ever varied, before which the nearer visions of the poet pause or move as does life itself before the ever varied universe that is its stage. He then discusses Tennyson's art in the use of metaphor, particularly in *In Memoriam*, where the cumulative force of all the background pictures and their value in the poem can hardly be overestimated.

Johnson, Edward Dudley Hume. *The Alien Vision of Victorian Poetry: Sources of the Poetic Imagination in Tennyson, Brown-*

ing, and Arnold. Princeton Studies in English, No. 34. Princeton: Princeton University Press, 1952.

"Tennyson," pp. 1-71, treats the theme of the sensitive and intellectual artist, living and writing during the transition from an organic to a critical social period. An understanding person in such a milieu must feel a conflict between the tendency to withdraw and the need to participate. Just as Tennyson avoided extremes in either direction, critics should balance their analyses.

Johnson, W. Stacy. "The Theme of Marriage in Tennyson," *The Victorian Newsletter,* No. 12 (Autumn 1957), 6-10.

True marriage in Tennyson represents the physically and spiritually fruitful life, and becomes a kind of counter theme to the Tennysonian ground-theme of loneliness and mortality. The development of this contrast can be traced from the early poems through the *Idylls,* and beyond.

Jones, Sir Henry. "Tennyson," *British Academy Proceedings,* IV (1909), 131-145.

Writing in 1909, Sir Henry Jones feels that Tennyson's fame will return. The problems of his age were in 1909 still active and critics will not accept an artist until the strain and the strife of actual experience is past. Jones stresses the "absolute originality of Tennyson's artistic touch" and "the absolute fidelity of his rendering of his age."

Ker, William Paton. *Tennyson.* Cambridge: Cambridge University Press, 1909. (The Leslie Stephen Lecture delivered in the Senate House, Cambridge, 11 November, 1909.)

A very original and perceptive estimate, written during the early years of the reaction.

Killham, John. *Critical Essays on the Poetry of Tennyson.* New York: Barnes and Noble, 1960. London: Routledge and Kegan Paul, 1960.

Excellent introduction in which Mr. Killham gives a review of modern criticism. He then divides the essays into seven groups:
I.   Tennyson in Temporal Contexts—The Victorian and The Modern.
    G. M. Young. *The Age of Tennyson.*
    Arthur J. Carr. *Tennyson as a Modern Poet.*
II. Tennyson in Artistic Contexts.
    H. M. McLuhan. *Tennyson and Picturesque Poetry.*
    H. M. McLuhan. *Tennyson and the Romantic Epic.*

III. Symbol and Myth—Modes of Indirection.
G. Robert Stange. *Tennyson's Garden of Art: a Study of the Hesperides.*
Elizabeth Hillman Waterston. *Symbolism in Tennyson's Minor Poems.*
Lionel Stevenson. *The 'High-born Maiden' Symbol in Tennyson.*
G. Robert Stange. *Tennyson's Mythology: a Study of Demeter and Persephone.*
IV. Variant Readings: I. *"Ulysses."*
W. W. Robson. *The Dilemma of Tennyson.*
E. J. Chiasson. *Tennyson's Ulysses—a Re-interpretation.*
II. *"Tears, Idle Tears."*
Cleanth Brooks. *The Motivation of Tennyson's Weeper.*
Graham Hough. *"Tears, Idle Tears."*
Leo Spitzer. *"Tears, Idle Tears" Again.*
V. *In Memoriam*
T. S. Eliot. *In Memoriam.*
VI. *Maud.*
John Killham. *Maud—the Function of the Imagery.*
VII. *Idylls of the King*—a Fresh View.
F. E. L. Priestley. *Tennyson's Idylls.*
Full bibliography in alphabetical order is given for these entries.

Kingsley, Charles. "Tennyson," *Fraser's Magazine*, XLII (September 1850), 245-255. Reprinted in *Miscellanies* I, pp. 214-233. London: John W. Parker, 1859.

Deals with Tennyson's work up to and including *In Memoriam*. This review is of value as showing the extraordinary position which Tennyson held in 1850 with "the cultivated young men" of the day, particularly at the universities.

Kishi, Shigetsugu. *Lafcadio Hearn's Lectures on Tennyson.* Tokyo: Hokuseido Press, 1941.

By "Hearn's last student in the Imperial University of Tokyo," based on notes taken at Hearn's lectures.

Kissane, James. "Victorian Mythology," *Victorian Studies*, VI (September 1962), 5-28.

Section IV, pp. 25-28, contains a study of Tennyson's use of the Demeter legend, emphasizing the Victorians' aesthetic and ethical approach to mythology. The success of Tennyson's treatment is the measure of a receptivity to legend which is one of his most sustaining resources as a poet.

Korg, Jacob. "The Pattern of Fatality in Tennyson's Poetry," *Victorian Newsletter*, No. 14 (Fall 1958), 8-11.

Stresses the swing of the pendulum from hope to despair, ripeness to decay, maturity to death, felicity followed by destruction and so on.

Lang, Andrew. *Alfred Tennyson*. Modern English Writers. New York: Dodd, Mead, 1901. Edinburgh, London: William Blackwood and Sons, 1901.

One of the most versatile Victorian men of letters makes a critical estimate of Tennyson and his poetry.

Langbaum, Robert. *The Poetry of Experience*. London: Chatto and Windus, 1957.

Pages 87-93 contain a study of Tennyson's use of the dramatic monologue, largely by comparing *St. Simeon Stylites* with Browning's *Johannes Agricola*. There are interesting references to other poems of Tennyson and Browning and to Eliot's *Waste Land*.

The Laughter of the Muses. Glasgow: Thomas Murray and Son, 1869.

A long and violent attack in rhymed couplets on the work of Tennyson and Browning, cleverly written and interesting in view of its date.

Leavis, F. R. *New Bearings in English Poetry*. London: Chatto and Windus, 1950.

Contains a brief and superficial reference to Tennyson, who is dismissed as characteristic of his time. "Victorian poetry admits that the actual world is alien, recalcitrant and unpoetical, and that no protest is worth making except the protest of withdrawal." Tennyson did his best to cope with the changing conditions of the time, but "to justify his ambition would have taken a much finer intelligence and a much more robust, original genius . . . much greater strength and courage."

Lucas, Frank Laurence. *Eight Victorian Poets*. London and New York: Macmillan, 1930.

The Introduction has great charm and great value for the present machine age. "Tennyson," pp. 1-21, lists the four main charges against Tennyson. In reply Mr. Lucas dwells on the beauty of phrase and background, the use of nature and the classics, the music of the verse.

Lucas, Frank Laurence. *Tennyson*. London: Longmans Green, 1957. Reprint 1961.

A short, critical biography, written in the usual delightful style of Mr. Lucas. Perhaps an under-estimation of the dynamic in Tennyson's personality and in his poetry.

Lucas, Frank Laurence. *Tennyson, Poetry and Prose.* Oxford: Clarendon Press, 1947.

Includes criticisms by the *Quarterly Review*, Edward Fitzgerald, Matthew Arnold, Sir Leslie Stephen, and Harold Nicolson. Introduction and notes are by Mr. Lucas. A very useful volume.

Luce, Morton. *Tennyson.* London: J. M. Dent, 1901.

After a brief introduction dealing with Tennyson's life and characteristics as thinker and poet, the book analyzes in detail the poems contained in his successive publications, including those printed for the first time in Hallam Tennyson's *Memoir*. The author writes with knowledge and understanding and his comment still has value.

MacEachen, Dougald B. "Tennyson and the Sonnet," *Victorian Newsletter*, No. 14 (Fall 1958), 1-8.

Tennyson did not adjust his talents to the requirements of the sonnet when those talents were at the height of their perfection. When he went back to it after a long interval, he used it only as a conventional measuring cup on a few special occasions.

Mackail, J. W. "Tennyson," in *Studies of English Poets.* London: Longmans Green and Co., 1926.

A short essay by a great classical scholar which carried the Tennyson revival a stage further than Nicolson had done. Contains an interesting comparison between the careers of Tennyson and Queen Victoria and concludes with an analysis which shows that Tennyson's place amongst the English classics, whose poetry is the permanent heritage of the whole English-speaking people, is assured.

Mackay, Eric. *Vox Clamantis.* London: W. Stewart and Co., n.d.

Aims to prove the Laureate a plagiarist in one poem by making "a comparison, analytical and critical, between *Columbus at Seville* of Joseph Ellis, 1869, and the *Columbus* of the Poet Laureate, 1880."

Macleod, W. B. *Lecture on the Genius of Alfred Tennyson.* London: Bean and Webley and Co., n.d.

Published at the request of Frederick Tennyson. Stresses purity of the poet's thought, sadness which pervades his work, his love of nature, his genius as a musical poet, his fancy, the patriotic element in his poetry, his view of society, his drama, his humour, and finally Tennyson as a religious teacher.

Magnus, Laurie. "Tennyson a Hundred Years After," *Cornhill Magazine* N.S., LXVI (June 1929), 660-670.

A valuable contribution to the revival. Analyzes Tennyson's position in relation to the thought of the 19th century and our own. In Tennyson's poems "the *anima mundi* is there, as well as the spirit of his age, captured in passage after passage of emotion remembered in tranquillity."

Mallock, W. H. *Atheism and the Value of Life*. London: Richard Bentley and Son, 1884.

The second essay in this volume, "Tennyson in the Shadow," is of surpassing interest. In it Mallock, one of the most brilliant of the sceptical minds of the late 19th century, surveys Tennyson's work up to and including his volume of 1880. The result is still fresh, stimulating, and illuminating. Referring to the 1880 volume, Mallock maintains that there is no deterioration of Tennyson's poetic powers, any change in his poetry being due to the change in the temper and circumstances of the time, to which his work inevitably reacts.

Marshall, George O., Jr. "Giftbooks, Tennyson, and *The Tribute* (1837)," *The Georgia Review* (Winter 1962), 459-464.

Stresses the importance of the majority of the contributors of *The Tribute* and sees evidence in it that a healthy poetical atmosphere prevailed in 1837. Also suggests that Tennyson may have been indebted for the name "Maud," if not for part of his story, to an anonymous ballad published in this volume.

McLuhan, H. M. "Tennyson and Picturesque Poetry," *Essays in Criticism*, I (July 1951), 262-282. In *Critical Essays*, ed. John Killham, pp. 67-85.

Discusses Arthur Hallam's review of Tennyson's *Poems, Chiefly Lyrical* in *Englishman's Magazine* (1831) and compares Hallam's propositions with the subsequent standpoints of Joyce, Yeats, Pound, and Eliot. Until 1842 Tennyson seems to have retained Hallam's insights exclusively. Thereafter he began to admit rhetoric and reflexion into his verse. The Victorians and Romantics, lacking the comprehensive and elastic technique of later poets (e.g. Baudelaire and Rimbaud), were compelled to keep to "the single picture-like perspective." An interesting and suggestive essay.

McLuhan, H. M. "Tennyson and the Romantic Epic," in *Critical Essays*, ed. John Killham, pp. 86-95.

Basing himself on J. W. Mackail's *Lectures on Greek Poetry*, McLuhan shows how, following the precedent of Theocritus, Tennyson applied the idyll form to lyric, epic, and dramatic poetry, and also to the poetry of reflexion and sentiment.

Moore, John Murray. *Three Aspects of the Late Alfred, Lord Tennyson*. Manchester: Marsden, 1901.

Three studies, read as papers for discussion at meetings of the Literary and Philosophical Society of Liverpool (England) in 1897 and 1898, treating Tennyson as Poet of Nature, National Poet, and Poet of Humanity.

Nicolson, Harold. *Tennyson: Aspects of His Life, Character, and Poetry*. London: Constable, 1923.

Climax of the reaction movement, brilliant in appreciation as well as in depreciation. Aroused interest and led to deeper study of Tennyson. The most influential study of the subject after the publication of H. J. C. Grierson's essay in the *Cambridge History of English Literature* and before T. S. Eliot's essay on *In Memoriam*.

Nicolson, Harold. "Tennyson: Fifty Years After," *Poetry Review*, XXXIII (November-December 1942), 333-336.

The essay repeats with little change the line adopted by the author in 1923, but the general tone is perhaps more appreciative. The last words are, "I look forward with confidence to a Tennyson revival."

Noel, Roden. "The Poetry of Tennyson," *Contemporary Review*, XLVII (February 1885), 202-224.

An appreciative survey by a poet and scholar of whose work Tennyson had a good opinion. Finds that "the dominant note of Tennyson's poetry is assuredly the delineation of human moods, modulated by nature and through a system of Natural Symbolism."

Noyes, Alfred. "Tennyson and Some Recent Critics," *Some Aspects of Modern Poetry*. London: Hodder and Stoughton, 1924.

An early and effective challenge to the reaction. "The plain truth is that a very large part of the recent depreciation of Tennyson comes from those who are quite unaware of the regions of thought in which he moved."

Noyes, Alfred. *Tennyson.* London: William Blackwood and Sons, 1932.
   A detailed analysis of Tennyson's place in literature. Noyes calls Tennyson "the clearest sighted critic of the characteristics of his age," a poet upholding great fundamental faiths while understanding modern science better than any other poet since Lucretius. The lack of insight lies with the critics, not with Tennyson. Also excellent discussion of Tennyson's poetic technique.

Noyes, Alfred. "The Real Tennyson," *Quarterly Review,* CCLXXXVII (October 1949), 495-507.
   A review of Sir Charles Tennyson's biography of the poet. Noyes emphasizes the fresh light thrown on many poems by the new facts disclosed in the biography.

Paden, W. D. *Tennyson in Egypt: a Study of the Imagery of His Earlier Work.* University of Kansas Humanistic Studies, No. 27. Lawrence: University of Kansas Press, 1942.
   A valuable study of the imagery in Tennyson's early work, and the development of his personality. Excellent notes, covering a very wide range.

Paul, Herbert. "Aspects of Tennyson, IV, the Classical Poems," *Nineteenth Century,* XXXIII (March 1893), 436-453.
   Careful study by an eminent publicist and scholar. One of a series of obituary articles probably commissioned by the editor, Tennyson's friend, Sir James Knowles.

Pitt, Valerie. *Tennyson Laureate.* London: Barrie and Rockliff, 1962.
   A study of the poet's development, based upon the tension between withdrawal and participation, or "between the insight of the solitary and the sense of the common and the social." Miss Pitt has an independent point of view which she states forcibly and defends capably, though perhaps not always convincingly. She deals trenchantly with Nicolson and Auden and crosses swords with Eliot, speaking out boldly for Tennyson's achievement as a "public Poet." Her book concludes as follows, "It is the measure of a poet that he expands the possibilities of the language. That Tennyson did so while creating and maintaining a poetic tradition which the first mass audience in the world would accept, and in which it found comfort, was in itself a considerable achievement. That he did so in a cultural situation unpropitious to literature, suggests an unusual greatness."

Postma, J. *Tennyson as Seen by His Parodists*. New York: Stechert, 1926. Amsterdam: H. J. Paris, 1926.

Parodies were written to criticize, often to reprove, never to praise, nearly all being on some particular poem or part of a poem, not on the poet's general style.

Preyer, Robert. "Tennyson as an Oracular Poet," *Modern Philology*, LV, No. 4 (May 1958), 239-251.

The thesis here is that Tennyson some time during the 1830's abandoned the "oracular" (transcendental or visionary) method of poetic composition, probably because he found that this was involving him in crucial moral and psychological difficulties, and turned to the writing of mundane domestic idylls and conversation pieces. An interesting, if highly controversial, contribution to an important but still inconclusive discussion. According to Dr. Preyer "oracular Poetry" is created by a search for fantastic beauty in the mindless depths of the psyche.

Priestley, F. E. L. "Tennyson," *University of Toronto Quarterly*, XXXII (October 1962-63), 102-106.

A review of J. H. Buckley's *Tennyson: The Growth of a Poet*. The review is as much a presentation of the author's views as a treatment of Buckley's book. Both are sufficiently important to deserve close study.

Pyre, James Francis Augustine. *The Formation of Tennyson's Style*. Madison: University of Wisconsin Press, 1921.

A study of Tennyson's prosody to the time of its highest perfection, the 1842 volume, some of the subjects being the period of imitation, experiments in metre, mastering blank verse, etc. Traces the development of Tennyson's style and prosody after 1830.

Quayle, William A. *Recovered Yesterdays in Literature*. New York: The Abingdon Press, 1916.

One chapter, "Tennyson's Men," pp. 88-144, classes men in Tennyson's poetry as (1) the men of fatal flaw, (2) the workers, (3) lovers, (4) religious men. Quotes passages from the poems. The article tends to be a bit sweet, not very deep.

Quiller-Couch, Sir A. T. "Tennyson in 1833," *The Poet as Citizen*. Cambridge: Cambridge University Press, 1934. Reprinted from *Times Literary Supplement*, September 14, 1933, p. 597.

A short article stressing the courage and determination with which Tennyson fought his way through the years following Arthur Hallam's death and the magnificence of the masterpiece (*In Memoriam*) which resulted.

Rand, Theodore H. "Limae Labor," *The McMaster University Journal*, I (June 1891), 1-11.

By presenting examples of Tennyson's revisions of his manuscripts, Mr. Rand illustrates the importance of polishing and perfecting in the art of poetry.

Robertson, J. M. "The Art of Tennyson," in *Essays Towards a Critical Method*. London: T. Fisher Unwin, 1889.

A very interesting study by a prominent Radical and Freethinker, who fully and brilliantly appreciates the achievement of the young and middle-aged Tennyson, but bitterly dislikes the political and social attitudes of the later volumes, and claims that in his later work, the poet, while retaining his old power of tragic and humorous characterization, has for the most part lost his power of creating rhythmic beauty.

Ryals, Clyde de L. *Theme and Symbol in Tennyson's Poems to 1850*. Philadelphia: University of Pennsylvania Press, 1964.

Follows Nicolson in holding that Tennyson's inner nature, as expressed in his early poetry, was "blended with the demands of his friends, his reviewers, his reading public, and, ultimately, of the *zeitgeist* itself," but differs from Nicolson in holding that the "Victorian" Tennyson was present in his poetry from the beginning, and that this interplay of the "real" and the "Victorian" gives the poems of this period (up to 1850) a special importance for 20th century man, who experiences many of the moral and spiritual confusions which faced Tennyson. The book has many interesting and valuable insights but needs to be read with discrimination.

Saintsbury, George. *A History of Nineteenth Century Literature*. London: Macmillan, 1896.

Pages 253-268 contain one of the most complete, concise and closely analyzed appraisals of Tennyson's achievement and place in our poetic hierarchy. The author concludes that Shakespeare, Spenser, Milton, and Shelley are greater poets, and that Wordsworth and Keats may be. But that no English poet has been so uniformly, and over such a large mass of work, exquisite, and that his versification is by far the most perfect of any English poet, resulting in a harmony positively incomparable. Perhaps pays too little attention to the deeper levels of Tennyson's achievement.

Saintsbury, George. *Periods of European Literature*. London and Edinburgh: William Blackwood, 1907.

The references to Tennyson in the sections entitled *The Romantic Triumph* and *The Later Nineteenth Century* deserve close consideration.

Saintsbury, George. "Tennyson," *Corrected Impressions*. London: Heinemann, 1895.

Finds Tennyson's chief merit in "an infinitely varied slow music and dreamy motion in lyric and that of concerted blank verse." Maintains that beauty will be discovered in his work "as long as the unknown laws which govern the presentations of beauty in sight and sound last."

Salt, Henry S. *Tennyson as a Thinker*. London: A. C. Fifield, 1909.

A typical work of the reaction. Finds Tennyson's philosophy "that of a man who, by the conditions of his birth, education, temperament and general surroundings, was to a large extent incapacitated for recognizing the true tendencies of the times in which he lived."

Sanders, Charles Richard. "Tennyson and the Human Hand," *Victorian Newsletter*, XI (Spring 1957), 5-13.

A very full analysis seeking to show how variously, extensively, and ingeniously Tennyson uses the human hand for the purpose of achieving continuity, development, artistic unity, and accumulated power.

Scaife, Christopher Henry Oldham. *Poetry of Alfred Tennyson: an Essay in Appreciation*. London: Cobden-Sanderson, 1930.

Made up of three lectures delivered in Cairo in 1930. The Foreword states that Tennyson has recovered his position with the critics but is generally regarded by the public with venomous indifference. The author seems to regard Nicolson and I'Anson Fausset as favourable critics, and his final paragraph says that Tennyson must be read in drastic selection, as a large part of his work must be condemned and much of the rest is only distinguished verse making.

S. G. G. "Browning and Tennyson," *Leisure Hour* (April 1890), 231-234.

An interesting comparison of the two poets.

Shepherd, Richard Herne. *Tennysoniana*. Second Edition. Revised and Enlarged. London: Pickering and Co., 1879.
    Partial bibliography of primary sources. Chapters on allusions to Holy Scriptures and classical writers, on Tennyson's versification, and on portraits of Tennyson.

Sidgwick, Arthur. *Tennyson*. London: Sidgwick and Jackson, 1909.
    A paper by an eminent classical scholar, read in the chapel of Trinity College, Cambridge, shortly after Tennyson's death.

Snow, Jane Elliott. *Women of Tennyson*. Buffalo, New York: The Wenborne-Summer Co., 1901.
    Quotations from Tennyson's poems which have a bearing upon women. Classified as living characters, women of history, ideal women, and mythical women.

Squire, Sir John. "Tennyson," *The London Mercury*, II (August 1920), 443-445.
    The opinions, both favourable and unfavourable, of an eminent poet, critic and editor, not so highly regarded now as in the 1920's.

Stevenson, Lionel. "The 'Highborn Maiden' Symbol in Tennyson," *PMLA*, LXIII (March 1948), 234-243. Reprinted in *Critical Essays*, ed. John Killham, pp. 126-136.
    Suggests that Tennyson derived this symbol from Shelley. Its persistent use in his poems suggests a psychological interpretation. Finds that the symbol "conforms with amazing precision to the theory of Jung regarding the archetypal image of the *anima*."

Stevenson, Lionel. "The Pertinacious Victorian Poets," *University of Toronto Quarterly*, XXI (April 1952), 232-245.
    Contains some perceptive comment on Tennyson and some useful references to current criticism.

Stevenson, Lionel, "Tennyson, Browning, and a Romantic Fallacy," *University of Toronto Quarterly*, XIII, No. 2 (January 1944), 175-185.
    Treats Shelley's influence on Tennyson; then shows that Tennyson turned from the abstract and based his ideas of the poet's function on the need to appeal to the ordinary sympathies of men.

Stirling, James Hutchinson. *Jerrold, Tennyson and Macaulay*. Edinburgh: Edmonston and Douglas, 1868.
    A good example of the eulogistic Victorian survey.

"A Study of Tennyson," *The Graphic*, May 7, 1870, pp. 538-539. (Signed "By an Architect.")
"A phrase of Tennyson's is sufficient to bring an English building before us." The essay makes a few comparisons of Tennyson's method with that of other English writers; also shows that Tennyson often presents architecture as the characters in the poems would have been the building—in a sort of architectural pathetic fallacy.

Swinburne, A. C. "Tennyson and Musset," *Miscellanies*. London: Chatto and Windus, 1886.
This essay is famous for Swinburne's rhapsody on Tennyson's *Rizpah* and his attack on "the Morte d'Albert or Idylls of the Prince Consort." It is worth study for the light which it throws on Swinburne as well as for the light which Swinburne throws on Tennyson.

Tainsh, Edward Campbell. *A Study of the Works of Alfred Tennyson*. London: Macmillan, 1893.
Useful index, good for reference. An entertaining discussion of this book between Arthur Waugh and the author will be found in *The Academy* (London), August 5 and September 2, 1893.

"Tennyson," *Times Literary Supplement*. August 5, 1909, p. 281.
Article celebrating the centenary of Tennyson's birth. Apparently by a friend of Hallam, Lord Tennyson as it quotes from the still unpublished *Devil and the Lady*. Cautiously eulogistic, showing clearly the effect of the reaction. Tennyson considered not a born story teller, an analyst not a creator of character. Suggests that the work included in the volumes of 1842 will prove the most enduring of his contributions. No mention of *In Memoriam* or the later philosophic poems. Praises Tennyson's "impeccable truth of observation, his never waning love of beauty, his devotion to an ideal of art from which he never deviated. These achievements place him among the great poets of his time."

Tennyson, Sir Charles. "The Dream in Tennyson's Poetry," *The Virginia Quarterly Review*, XL, No. 2 (Spring 1964), 228-248.
The writer emphasizes the very important part which the dream plays in Tennyson's poetry as a source of image, simile, and metaphor, and even as a vital element in the poetic structure. He attributes this to the poet's lifelong occupation with

Neo-Platonic ideas about the ideal (spiritual) and the phenomenal (material). The writer takes this opportunity to repair an omission from the essay which should have included a reference to the opening stanza of Section 71 of *In Memoriam* where Tennyson clearly refers to dream, death, trance and even madness as possible channels of communication with the spiritual reality.

Tennyson, Sir Charles. *Six Tennyson Essays.* London: Cassell and Co. 1954.

Very full treatment of Tennyson's humour, politics, religion, versification, some of the manuscripts of the *Idylls of the King,* a note on Tennyson as a narrative poet, and note on reading his poetry.

Tillotson, Kathleen. "Rugby 1850: Arnold, Clough, Walrond, and 'In Memoriam'," *Review of English Studies,* N.S., IV (April 1953), 122-140.

Beginning with a scene from A. G. Butler's *The Three Friends: a Story of Rugby in the Forties,* Dr. Tillotson skilfully analyzes Arnold's reactions to Tennyson's poetry.

Traill, H. D. "Aspects of Tennyson, I" *Nineteenth Century,* XXXII (December 1892), 952-966.

One of a series of careful obituary articles by distinguished contemporaries, probably commissioned by the editor, Tennyson's friend Sir James Knowles.

Van Dyke, Henry J., Jr. *An Introduction to the Poems of Tennyson.* Boston: Ginn, the Athenaeum Press, 1903.

Calls Tennyson the most representative poet of the 19th century and endeavours to show in 93 pages the growth of his mind and art, the methods which he followed, the variety of his work, and the chief qualities which mark his poetry.

Van Dyke, Henry J., Jr. "Milton and Tennyson," *Presbyterian Review,* IV, No. 16 (October 1883), xvi and 437.

Classes Milton and Tennyson as the two great religious poets of England, placing Milton as one of the six or perhaps four greatest poets of the world. Tennyson is in the highest rank of the poets immediately below these. The author proceeds to show the real intellectual and moral kinship of the two poets and the profound analogy in their works "which has hitherto escaped the notice of the critics." A careful study worth reading.

Van Dyke, Henry J., Jr. *The Poetry of Tennyson*. New York: Charles Scribner's, 1898. Tenth edition revised and enlarged. Praises Tennyson's delicate, vague yet potent lyrical power and his spiritual courage. He is the poet of faith. In the appendix is a useful chronology and a list of Biblical references. See also a new edition, revised and enlarged. London: Elkin Mathews, 1906.

"Virgil and Tennyson," *Quarterly Review*, CXCIII (January 1901), 99-129.
A full and careful comparison of the two poets, relating life, background, and achievement.

Ward, William G. *Tennyson's Debt to Environment*. Boston: Roberts Bros., 1898.
A brief and eulogistic survey characteristic of the age before the reaction.

Warren, Sir Thomas Herbert. *The Centenary of Tennyson, 1809-1909*. Oxford: Clarendon Press, 1909.
A lecture given to University Extension students in the Sheldonian Theatre, August 6, 1909. A tribute, honoring the poet on the hundredth anniversary of his birth, by the President of Magdalen College, Oxford. Warren was a close friend of Tennyson's during his last years.

Waterston, Elizabeth Hillman. "Symbolism in Tennyson's Minor Poems," *University of Toronto Quarterly*, XX (July 1951), 369-380. In *Critical Essays*, ed. John Killham, pp. 113-125.
Suggests that in his minor poems Tennyson made a consistent effort to fuse the direct and oblique methods of symbolic writing.

Webb, W. Trego. "The Rhythm of Tennyson," *Calcutta Review*, CCIII (January 1896), 1-13.
Deals with the effect of metre and sound in Tennyson's rhythm. A useful study in a field which has not been fully worked.

Whitman, Walt. "A Word About Tennyson," in *Complete Prose Works*, pp. 403-405. Boston: Small, Maynard and Co. London: G. P. Putnam's Sons, 1898.
Begins with a comparison of *Locksley Hall* and *Locksley Hall Sixty Years After*. "Tennyson is not to be mentioned as a rugged, evolutionary, aboriginal force . . . but he has been consistent throughout with the native, healthy, patriotic special element and promptings of himself. His moral line is

local and conventional but it is vital and genuine—his glove is a glove of silk, but his hand is a hand of iron. . . . As to his non-democracy, it fits him well and I like him the better for it. . . . Alfred Tennyson's is a superb character and will help give illustriousness through the long roll of time to our nineteenth century." A very important statement deserving detailed study.

Willey, Basil. "Tennyson," in *More Nineteenth Century Studies*. London: Chatto and Windus, 1956.

Sets Tennyson's life and work (up to 1850) against the background of his personal life and the times through which he lived. Sound, thorough and understanding. The author has wide knowledge and a keen sense of poetic values. One of the best short surveys of this century.

Wilson, Charles. "Mirror of a Shire: Tennyson's Dialect Poems," *Durham University Journal*, LII (December 1959), 22-28.

After an able discussion of their background, Mr. Wilson says of the dialect poems, "They are, to my mind, unique not only among Tennyson's own poetry but in English poetry as a whole. Save for Chaucer, no one has portrayed bucolic life with technique so consummate or knowledge so intimate."

Wolfe, Humbert. *Tennyson*. The Poets on the Poets, No. 3. London: Faber and Faber, 1930.

Though short (only 60 octavo pages) this is an important work in the Tennyson revival. The author concentrates on a detailed critical study of *Maud* in order "to prove by a single example that much recent criticism was the result rather of reaction against Victorianism than of reading the poet." The author's biographical assumptions will hardly stand up against the results of recent research, and his treatment of the *Idylls* and later poems is sketchy and superficial, but the book is brilliantly written and full of valuable insights.

Young, G. M. *The Age of Tennyson*. Oxford: Oxford University Press, 1939. (Warton Lecture on English Poetry.) In *Critical Essays*, ed. John Killham, pp. 25-40.

A penetrating study by a veteran critic who had lived through the reaction and the early years of the revival.

11

Critical and Interpretative: Specific Volumes and Major Poems

POEMS, CHIEFLY LYRICAL (1830)

[Bowring, Sir John.] "Tennyson's Poems," *Westminster Review*, XIV (January-April 1831), 210-224. Review of Tennyson's volume *Poems, Chiefly Lyrical*.

Bowring (1792-1872) to whom this review has been attributed, was a distinguished linguist and traveller who at one time planned a history, with translated examples, of the popular poetry both of the Western and Eastern world. The review is enthusiastically, even extravagantly, favourable, but concludes with a warning to the young poet against too great an indulgence of his fancy and facility. According to W. D. Paden, "Tennyson and the Reviewers (1829-1835)," this review was by William Johnson Fox, editor of the *Monthly Repository*. Fox gave a very favourable review to Tennyson's 1833 volume, *Poems*.

Hunt, Leigh. Review of *Poems, Chiefly Lyrical*, *Tatler*, February 24, 1831, pp. 593 594; February 26, 1831, pp. 601-602.

Leigh Hunt reviewed both Tennyson's volume and Charles Tennyson's small volume, *Sonnets and Fugitive Pieces*. The tone of the reviews was indicated by the statement, "We have great pleasure in stating that we have seen no such poetical writing since the last volume of Mr. Keats."

Marshall, George O., Jr. "Tennyson's 'The Poet': Mis-seeing Shelley Plain," *Philological Quarterly*, XL (January 1961), 156-157.

Points out that Tennyson's *The Poet* was written before the publication of Shelley's *Defence of Poetry* (1820) from which several critics had considered it derived.

Mill, J. S. Review of *Poems, Chiefly Lyrical, Westminster Review* (January 1831). Reprinted in *Famous Reviews*, ed. R. B. Johnson. London, New York and Melbourne: Isaac Pitman and Sons, 1911.

Emphasizes the originality of the poems, but expresses some apprehension that Tennyson's peculiar gifts may "degrade him into a poetical harlequin." "He has higher work to do than that of disporting himself among 'mystics' and 'flowing philosophers.'"

Strout, Alan Lang. "Croker and Tennyson Again," *Notes and Review of English Studies*, XIV (October 1938), 428-439.

Analyzes the famous review of *Poems, Chiefly Lyrical* by John Wilson ("Christopher North") and Wilson's subsequent reference to Tennyson and comes to the conclusion that Wilson was guilty rather of inability to comprehend the new than of premeditated malice. A useful study.

Strout, Alan Lang. "Croker and Tennyson Again," *Notes and Queries*, CXCII (July 1947), 317-318; (November 1947), 498-499.

The first contribution prints in full Crocker's letter of resignation to Lockhart, which gives as one of the writer's reasons the favourable review given by the *Quarterly* to Tennyson's poems of 1842. The second contribution prints Croker's letter of Jan. 27, 1833, sending in the final script of his famous attack on *Poems, Chiefly Lyrical*.

Wilson, J. (Christopher North). Review of *Poems, Chiefly Lyrical, Edinburgh Blackwood's Magazine*, XXXI (May 1832), 721-741. Reprinted in *Essays Critical and Imaginative*, II (1866), and see "Christopher North on Tennyson," *Review of English Studies*, XIV (1938), 428-439.

This was the review that provoked Tennyson's epigram *To Christopher* in *Poems* (1833) and brought down on him the disastrous review of that volume by J. W. Croker in *The Quarterly Review*.

POEMS (1833)

[Croker, John Wilson.] Review of *Poems* (1833), *Quarterly Review*, XLIX (April 1833), 81-96.

This violently prejudiced and unscrupulous review by the author of the notorious attack in the same review on Keats' *Endymion* undoubtedly had a very adverse effect on Tennyson's reputation during the 1830's and helped to delay his next publication. The review was often attributed to Lockhart, but Sir H. J. C. Grierson (*Times Literary Supplement*, April 24, 1937) disproved this.

[Forster, John.] Review of *Poems* (1833), *True Sun*, January 19, 1833, p. [3].
This very favourable anonymous review was almost certainly by Forster, who later became one of Tennyson's closest friends and most influential supporters.

Fox, William Johnson. Review of Tennyson's volumes of 1830 and 1833 in *The Monthly Repository*, N.S., VII (January 1833), 30-41.
Fox was editor of *The Monthly Repository* and one of the few critics to write favourably of Browning's *Pauline*, which also came out in 1833. Fox discussed Tennyson's work from the point of view of philosophical content and artistry and expressed the opinion that he had a large endowment of both these qualities, "yielding, perhaps, among poets of modern fame, only to Wordsworth in the one, and only to Coleridge in the other." Fox is thought by some critics to have been the author of the notice in the *Westminster Review* of *Poems, Chiefly Lyrical*, generally attributed to Sir John Bowring.

Mill, John Stuart. Review of *Poems, Chiefly Lyrical* and *Poems* (1833), *London Review*, I (July 1835), 402-424.
One of the few favourable reviews between the publication of Croker's notice in the *Quarterly* and the issue of the two volumes of 1842. Mill's emphasis on the deficiencies still observable in Tennyson's versification may have reinforced the poet's struggle during the years 1833-1842 to improve his poetic technique.

POEMS (1842)

Forster, John. Review of *Poems*, 1842, *Examiner*, May 28, 1842, pp. 340-341.
The first review of the 1842 volumes to appear. An almost uniformly eulogistic survey by a very influential critic.

Milnes, R. M. (Baron Houghton). *Westminster Review*, XXXVIII (October 1842), 371-390.
Review of *Poems*, 1842, by one of the several critics who emphasized that "the function of the poet in this day of

ours" was "to teach still more than he delights." Milnes was a close friend of the poet from Cambridge days.

Spedding, James. *Edinburgh Review*, LXXVII (April 1843), 373-391. Reprinted in *Reviews and Discourses*. London: Kegan Paul, 1879.

    Review of *Poems*, 1842. Spedding was one of Tennyson's closest friends. His review of the two volumes of 1842 would undoubtedly have been more favourable but for editorial policy. It deals in great detail with *The Palace of Art, St. Simeon Stylites, The Two Voices,* and *The Vision of Sin,* on the ground that these poems, though they may not show the author's art in its most perfect or attractive form, show the depth from which it springs. "Powers are displayed in these volumes, adequate to the production of a very great work. At least we should find it difficult to say which of the requisite powers is wanting." In the *Edinburgh Review* the word "very" was struck out by the editor. A very important essay.

Sterling, John. Review of *Poems*, 1842, *Quarterly Review*, LXX (September 1842), 385-416. Reprinted in *Essays and Tales* by John Sterling, edited by Julius C. Hare. London: John W. Parker, 1848.

    Sterling was a close friend of the poet and his review, which was favourable, would have been more so but for restrictions imposed by his editor. Sterling's treatment of *Morte d'Arthur* was one of the factors which caused Tennyson to postpone his projected attempt to compose an epic on the Arthurian legends.

W. A. C. "Poems by Alfred Tennyson," *London University Magazine*, I (December 1842), 286-314.

    A review of the volumes of 1842. A good example of a detailed, eulogistic and not very discriminating survey. Tentatively attributed to William Arthur Case by Edgar Shannon (see *Tennyson and the Reviewers*).

THE PRINCESS

Dawson, G. E. *A Study, with Critical and Explanatory Notes, of Alfred Tennyson's "The Princess."* Montreal: Dawson Brothers, 1882.

    A long and careful introductory study is followed by some useful notes. Dawson concludes that *The Princess*, as a work of art, is the most complete and satisfying of all Tennyson's works.

The introduction includes a useful summary of contemporary criticism. Though Dawson's estimate runs counter to current evaluations, he probably understood Tennyson's *intentions* better than any other critic. (See letter from Tennyson to Dawson quoted in Hallam Tennyson's *Memoir*, I, 256.)

Killham, John. *Tennyson and The Princess*. London: The Athlone Press, 1958.
Excellent treatment, much new material, throwing light on the sources and background of many of Tennyson's ideas and conclusions in *The Princess* and *In Memoriam*.

Millhauser, Milton. "Tennyson's *Princess* and *Vestiges*," *PMLA*, LXIX (March 1954), 337-343.
Discusses the possible influence on Tennyson of the publication of Chambers' *Vestiges of Creation* in 1844.

Ryals, Clyde de L. "The 'Weird Seizures' in *The Princess*," *Texas Studies in Literature and Language*, IV, 2 (Summer 1962), 268-275.
An acute study of an important subject which has received little worthwhile consideration.

Tennyson, Charles. "Tennyson Papers: IV. The Making of *The Princess*," *Cornhill Magazine*, CLIII, No. 918 (June 1936), 672-680.
Notes on "the extant manuscript of *The Princess*, throwing light upon Tennyson's method of composition at the zenith of his powers."

Wallace, Percy M. *Tennyson: The Princess*, with introduction and notes. London and New York: Macmillan and Co., 1892.
Prepared primarily for Indian students but the introduction and notes are thorough and sensible and may still be of use. The editor states that the proofs were submitted to Hallam Tennyson who supplied some notes, enclosed in brackets and signed "H. T."

IN MEMORIAM

Beeching, Henry Charles. *"In Memoriam" with an Analysis and Notes*. London: Methuen, 1923.
Analysis not so good as Bradley's. Notes interesting.

Bose, A. *Tennyson's "In Memoriam." A Revaluation.* Calcutta: General Printers and Publishers, 1953.

A useful and suggestive study, written with insight and knowledge of the background. There is a useful appendix on the reviews of *In Memoriam.*

Bradley, Andrew Cecil. *A Commentary on Tennyson's "In Memoriam."* London and New York: Macmillan, 1901.

The standard analysis and commentary on *In Memoriam.* Its purpose is to show the bearing of the sections on one another and to deal with difficulties of interpretation.

Chapman, Elizabeth Rachel. *A Companion to "In Memoriam."* London: Macmillan, 1888.

A section by section paraphrase, said to have been approved by the poet.

Davidson, Thomas. *Prolegomena to "In Memoriam."* With an index to the poem. Boston: D. C. Heath, 1897.

His aim is "to bring out into clearness the religious soul-problem which forms its unity." William James of Harvard pronounced Thomas Davidson one of the profoundest thinkers and most learned men of the nineteenth century. The analysis is ample and excellent.

Dixon, James Main. "*The Rubaiyat* and *In Memoriam*," *Methodist Review*, CIV (May 1921), 353-368.

A comparison of the poets as well as of the poems. Perhaps more interesting about Fitzgerald than about Tennyson.

Dixon, James Main. *The Spiritual Meaning of "In Memoriam."* New York: Abingdon Press, 1920.

An interpretation; introduction by James Campbell.

Eliot, T. S. "*In Memoriam*," *Essays Ancient and Modern.* London: Faber and Faber, 1936. In *Critical Essays*, ed. John Killham, pp. 207-215.

Should be studied in relation to this poem though it also deals with Tennyson's total production.

Ellmann, Mary Joan. "Tennyson: Revision of *In Memoriam*, Section 85" *Modern Language Notes*, LXV (January 1950), 22-30.

By comparing the published version of Section 85 of *In Memoriam*, "Whatever way my life incline," with the MS version in J. M. Heath's Commonplace Book (Fitzwilliam

Museum, Cambridge), the author shows that several stanzas of the section were composed much earlier than generally assumed. "The comparison . . . indicates the futility of resting very much of the history of the composition of *In Memoriam* on internal evidence."

Enid and Nimue. Guildford: A. C. Curtis, 1902. London: Astolat Press, 1902.

A reprint of the trial book printed by Moxon's for Tennyson in 1857 from the copy in the British Museum.

Foakes, R. A. *The Romantic Assertion*. London: Methuen, 1958.

Contains, on pp. 111-138, a study of *In Memoriam*, under the subtitle, "The Rhetoric of Faith." After a useful analysis of the poem, the author emphasizes Tennyson's concern at the growing antagonism between science and religion and the lagging of spiritual behind material progress. Tennyson "desired to have the certainty that human life was advancing towards some goal, he wanted to believe, to Christianize his love for Hallam, but he found no solution to his problem, and his final reassurance stems not from a renewal of faith in God, but from a renewal of faith in love."

Gatty, Alfred. *A Key to Tennyson's "In Memoriam."* London: George Bell and Sons, 1885.

The author had known both Arthur Hallam and Edmund Lushington at school. Tennyson had "glanced" at an early edition of the "key" and made some invaluable corrections. The volume contains a commentary on every section of the poem and some useful notes. It is worth study.

Genung, John F. *Tennyson's "In Memoriam": Its Purpose and Structure*. Boston: Houghton Mifflin, 1884.

Relates *In Memoriam* to the age in which it was written and the growth of the poet's mind, compares it with *Lycidas* and *Adonais*, and outlines its structure.

Grandsen, K. W. *Tennyson: "In Memoriam,"* Studies in English Literature, No. 22. London: Edward Arnold, 1964.

A detailed study of great value, based on the author's conviction that Tennyson was "a highly conscious and self-conscious artist, and a man of the highest intelligence and sensibility." Mr. Gransden's Epilogue concludes, "Man's capacity to understand his limitations, to grasp his predicament, and to place it in a larger context of human development, began to decline during the last decades of the nineteenth century. The visionary power and the steadfastness began to fade. One sees this clearly in Arnold, prophet of modern *angst*. Lines like

> Still the same ocean round us raves
> But we stand still and watch the waves

express the static nature of modern impotence, and emphasize by contrast the way in which, in *In Memoriam*, the human spirit is still asserting itself against time and space, doubt and despair. It is a historical document from a time when the odds against man were heavy but not overwhelming. The artist still had 'a conscience and an aim,' wanting to teach because his readers wanted to learn. Though enmeshed in a new complex of scientific data Tennyson could still, without either ignoring or being ignorant of these data, speculate on man's spiritual nature with something of the old traditional grandeur. Our own age is overwhelmed with data which seem beyond assimilation and impossible to ignore. Tennyson is, if we like, the last great poet to link those soon to be notorious two cultures which now threaten to diminish the stature of man."

Grant, Stephen Allen. "The Mystical Implications of *In Memoriam*," *Studies in English Literature*, II, No. 4 (Autumn 1962), 401-495.

A valuable study. Tennyson's mysticism (which included genuine mystical experience) was both a determining force and an inspiration in his life as a poet. The ignorance of critics as to the true meaning of the mystic experience has led to the misinterpretation of his resolution to *In Memoriam* and his convictions about the universe. Worth careful study.

Holmes, Mabel Dodge. *The Poet as Philosopher; a Study of Three Philosophical Poems: "Nosce Teipsum," "The Essay on Man," "In Memoriam."* Philadelphia: University of Pennsylvania Press, 1921.

Discusses whether a poet can be an original philosopher, and concludes that the poet becomes a mouthpiece of other men's thoughts. His art, feeling, interpretation, and application are his own, but he is not an original thinker; he reflects his climate of opinion, Tennyson thus reflecting contemporary scientific thought.

Hough, Graham. "The Natural Theology of *In Memoriam*," *Review of English Studies*, XXIII (July 1947), 244-256.

A full and judicious analysis of the contemporary movements of thought by which Tennyson was probably influenced.

Dr. Hough finds three important elements: "The influence of science, transmitted especially through Lyell's *Geology;* the influence of Coleridge, experienced at Cambridge; and Tennyson's own religious intuitions, based ultimately on an unanalysable but completely cogent mystic experience." Worth careful study.

House, Humphrey. *"In Memoriam," All in Due Time.* London: Rupert Hart-Davis, 1955, pp. 130-139.

House joins with those who find that it is the fears and terrors of the speculative parts of *In Memoriam* which achieve the most satisfying poetic expression and that the optimistic progressive view of the world and life which ultimately triumphs in the poem, is correspondingly shallow, even emotionally dishonest. He concludes that the true development of the poem lies less in the passages of positive optimistic assertion than in those moments of achieved happiness and hope, in which the optimistic evolutionary philosophy is not described but taken for granted. The poem does contain the record of a deep and genuine transposition of mood from despair to acceptance and hope, and we can let all the oversimplified argument and the facile political optimism go and hold to such passages as the ending of section CXII and the last part of the Epithalamium.

Jennings, James George. *An Essay on Metaphor in Poetry.* With an appendix on the use of metaphor in Tennyson's *In Memoriam.* London: Blackie and Son, 1915. Discusses the use of metaphor in *In Memoriam.*

Johnson, E. D. H. "*In Memoriam:* The Way of the Poet," *Victorian Studies,* II (December 1958), 139-148.

The aim of this paper is "to show, first, that Bradley's schematization lends itself equally well to a formal analysis of the evolution of the Tennyson poetic, and secondly, that the process of philosophical and aesthetic growth exhibited in the poem are so interrelated in their successive phases as ultimately to be inseparable."

Kendall, J. L. "A Neglected Theme in Tennyson's *In Memoriam,*" *Modern Language Notes,* LXXVI (May 1961), 414-420.

The neglected theme, of which the importance is stressed, is that of failure and defeat.

Mattes, Eleanor Bustin. *In Memoriam, the Way of a Soul.* New York: Exposition Press, 1951.

Yale dissertation. Attempts to date sections of *In Memoriam*. Shows influence of nineteenth century ideas on Tennyson's thought in *In Memoriam*. An excellent guide to the sources and structure of the poem.

Metzger, Lore. "The Eternal Process: Some Parallels Between Goethe's *Faust* and Tennyson's "*In Memoriam*," *Victorian Poetry*, I, No. 3 (August 1963), 189-196.
A useful summary.

Meynell, Alice Christiana. "*In Memoriam*" *by Alfred Lord Tennyson*, with an analysis by the Rev. F. W. Robertson and an introduction by Alice Meynell. London: Blackie and Son, 1904.
The introduction is stimulating though rather ambivalent. See Robertson's analysis.

Moore, Carlisle. "Faith, Doubt and Mystical Experience in *In Memoriam*," *Victorian Studies*, VII, No. 2 (December 1963), 155-169.
"Few long poems achieve such a synthesis of disparate parts. During the long period of its composition Tennyson gained not only artistic development but religious and emotional maturity . . . along with the many strands of thought and feeling . . . there is the clear strand of mystical experience." A penetrating and valuable study.

Moore, John Robert. "Sources of *In Memoriam* in Tennyson's Early Poems," *Modern Language Notes*, XXXI (May 1916), 307-309.
Notes the occurrence in the three irregular sonnets entitled *Love* in *Poems Chiefly Lyrical* of ideas which occupy a prominent place in *In Memoriam*.

Moxon, Thomas Allen. *Tennyson's "In Memoriam": Its Message to the Bereaved and Sorrowful*. London: Skeffington, 1918.
A series of sermons preached at the church of St. Anne's, Soho, London, in the summer of 1917.

Robertson, The Rev. Frederick W. *Analysis of Mr. Tennyson's "In Memoriam."* London: Smith Elder and Co., 1862. Fifteenth edition, 1901.
Has some importance as the work of an eminent preacher and divine who was a contemporary of the poet.

Rolfe, W. J. "Notes on Tennyson's *In Memoriam*," *Poet-Lore*, VII (August-September 1895), 428-435.
Contains some valuable miscellaneous information.

Rosenberg, John D. "The Two Kingdoms of *In Memoriam*," *Journal of English and Germanic Philology*, LVIII (April 1959), 228-240.
　　An intelligent and valuable study. The "Two Kingdoms" are "two great myths," the myth of Progress and the Christian vision of the Kingdom of Heaven. *In Memoriam* is an effort "to unite evolutionary science and Christian faith."

Ryals, Clyde de L. "The Heavenly Friend": the New Mythos of "*In Memoriam*," *The Personalist*, XLIII (Summer 1962), 383-402.
　　The least successful of Mr. Ryal's important essays of the 1960's, particularly in the suggestion that Tennyson made a Christ figure of Hallam. There are excellent points made, but there are better analyses of *In Memoriam*.

Sparrow, John Hanbury Angus. *In Memoriam*. London: Nonesuch Press, 1933.
　　In his introduction Sparrow (now Warden of All Souls College, Oxford) classes Tennyson as "one of the greatest poets who has written in the English language," and *In Memoriam* as his greatest poem and "one of the most beautiful poems in the English language." Its chief appeal does not lie in its philosophy—Tennyson's lack of intellectual power prevented him from thinking things out—but for its poetry, that of a great poet "writing in the fullness of his powers under the influence of the deepest emotion he had ever felt."

Stevenson, The Rev. Morley. *Spiritual Teaching of Tennyson's "In Memoriam."* London: Wells, Gardner, and Darton, 1904.
　　Based on a series of sermons by the author. Claims Tennyson as a believer in the Incarnation. His "special contribution to religious thought does not lie in the fresh exposition of theological subtleties so much as in the reiteration and enforcement of certain fundamental and central beliefs."

IDYLLS OF THE KING

Boas, Frederick Samuel. "*Idylls of the King* in 1921," *Nineteenth Century*, XC (November 1921), 819-830.
　　While admitting that Tennyson's treatment of the Arthurian story necessitated an illegitimate transvaluation of some parts and leads to some insoluble entanglements, maintains that this is not only lawful, but of the very essence of Tennyson's genius, producing at its best poetry as timeless as that of Spenser or

Milton. An intelligent and careful study by a fine scholar, remarkable for its date, but perhaps to some extent influenced by the still potent reaction.
(Also printed in the Transactions of the Royal Society of Literature. "Essays by Divers Hands," II (1922), 23-43.)

Bradley, A. C. *Oxford Lectures on Poetry.* See under *Critical and Interpretative: General.*

Burchell, S. C.. "Tennyson's 'Allegory in the Distance,'" *PMLA*, LXVIII (June 1953), 418-424.
The phrase "allegory in the distance" was used by Benjamin Jowett with reference to the *Idylls* of 1859. In this interesting essay the author describes the *Idylls* "not as a unified poem but as a truly suggestive one, not locked in one dogmatic principle of Soul versus Body, but a medley of pure and symbolic narrative—a revelation, a diagnosis and a lament for modern life in its complexity and its decadence."

Cheetham, S. "The Arthurian Legends in Tennyson," *Contemporary Review*, VII (April 1868), 497-514.
Compares Tennyson's *Idylls* with the source passages in Malory, emphasizing the improvements introduced by him.

Cross, Tom Peete. "Alfred Tennyson as a Celticist," *Modern Philology*, XVIII (January 1921), 149-156.
A full and careful study of the sources of *Idylls of the King.* Tennyson responded as heartily to the early nineteenth-century revival of Celtic antiquities as he did to other phases of contemporary investigation, and "made an honest effort to ground his *Idylls* on the most reputable authorities of his day."

Davies, Samuel D. "Shakespeare's Miranda and Tennyson's Elaine," *Poet-Lore*, V (January 1893), 15-25.
An interesting comparison which illustrates the respective periods in which the two poets wrote as well as the attitude of the poets themselves.

Dawson, Canon. "The Morals of the Round Table," *Chambers's Journal*, XIII (November 1910), 781-784.
Malory's *Morte d'Arthur* is compared with the *Idylls of the King*, each being presented as the product of its age; but the story of Arthur remains the same ever, "the deathless struggle of men of good will against the meanness and cruelty of the world."

Dhaleine, L. *A Study on Tennyson's "Idylls of the King"*. Bar-le-duc: Comte-Jacquet, Facduel, 1905.

Interesting as a thesis for a French doctorate, otherwise not of much value.

Elsdale, Henry. *Studies in the "Idylls"*. London: Henry S. King and Co., 1878.

A study of Tennyson's poem made before the publication of *Balin and Balan*. While emphasizing Tennyson's poetic power and high ideals, the author finds an "absence of general solidarity" and of "a consistent, clearly defined programme of action and character." While realizing that the Idylls have an allegorical basis, Elsdale thinks this should have been given "a far better, more definite, consistent and uniform rendering."

Engbretsen, Nancy M. "The Thematic Evolution of *The Idylls of the King*," *Victorian Newsletter*, No. 26 (Fall 1964), 1-5.

Contains a stimulating, but not always convincing, comparison with the *Idylls* of a number of poems not usually regarded as relevant to them. In the *Idylls*, Tennyson transforms his frequently employed technique of mythic narrative into "a vehicle of oblique, highly contemporary, social and moral evaluation."

Gibbs, Lincoln R. "Tennyson's *Idylls of the King*," *Methodist Review*, XCV (September-October 1913), 756-763.

A valuable short study: sees Tennyson's poem as extending the charm and consecration of poetry to the organic life of the state.

Hartman, Joan E. "The Manuscripts of Tennyson's 'Gareth and Lynette,'" *Harvard Library Bulletin*, XIII (Spring 1959), 239-264.

A valuable study of Tennyson's methods based on two MS notebooks in the Harvard College Library.

Jones, Richard. *The Growth of the Idylls of the King*. Philadelphia: J. B. Lippincott, 1895.

One of the best books on the *Idylls*. Discusses subject-matter, including Tennyson's use of sources and rather full reference to Goethe's *Faust;* Tennyson's variations and revisions of early copies, and finally variations in the completed *Idylls*.

Kemble, J. T. "Tennyson's Arthurian Poem," *Spectator*, January 1, 1870, pp. 1-12.

Written by a close friend of the poet. Clear insight into the symbolic value of the *Idylls of the King*, written at a time when this interpretation was not general.

Knowles, James. "The Meaning of Mr. Tennyson's *King Arthur*," *Contemporary Review*, XXI (May 1873), 938-948.
An early exploration of the symbolism of the Idylls, no doubt based on the author's many talks with Tennyson on the subject.

Knowles, James. "Tennyson's Arthurian Poem," *Spectator*, January 1, 1870, pp. 15-17. Reprinted in *Tennyson and His Friends*. London: Macmillan, 1911.
Emphasizes symbolic element in the *Idylls* which were still without *Gareth and Lynette* and *Balin and Balan*. According to Hallam, Lord Tennyson (*Tennyson and his Friends*, p. 498). Knowles' letter was written after a talk which he had with the poet.

Littledale, Harold. *Essays on Lord Tennyson's 'Idylls of the King.'* London: Macmillan and Co., 1907. First edition 1893.
"The object of this book is to present a convenient summary of much information that is dispersed through too many books to be accessible at first hand in the case of the general reader." Traces sources, has an excellent chapter on each *Idyll*. Is one of the best commentaries on the *Idylls of the King*.

Ludlow, J. M. "Moral Aspects of Mr. Tennyson's *Idylls of the King*," *Macmillan's Magazine*, I (November 1859), 63-72.
A "dated" approach to the *Idylls*: "Love, its diseases and its counterfeits, such may be said to be the theme of the new volume." The poet here goes "straight home to the heart of the great mass of his countrymen, by broad pictures of human pathos, and clear exhibitions of lofty purpose."

Macaulay, G. C. *The Holy Grail*. With introduction and notes. London: Macmillan, 1893.
A valuable and thorough treatment by a fine scholar, who edited in uniform volumes *Gareth and Lynette*, *The Marriage of Geraint* and *Geraint and Enid*.

Macaulay, G. C. Tennyson, "*Gareth and Lynette*." Edited with introduction and notes. London and New York: Macmillan, 1893.
A useful edition. The Introduction includes a comparison of Tennyson's methods with those of Virgil and Spenser.

Macaulay, G. C. *Tennyson, "The Marriage of Geraint"* and *"Geraint and Enid."* Edited with introduction and notes. London and New York: Macmillan, 1892.

The introduction includes a summary of the tale in the *Mabinogion* on which Tennyson founded the two Idylls.

MacCallum, M. W. *Tennyson's Idylls of the King and Arthurian Story from the XVIth Century.* Glasgow: James Maclehose, 1894.

The introduction contains a full and scholarly account of the development and literary adaptation of the Arthurian legends through the centuries. The study of Tennyson's *Idylls* is the most complete yet written. Particularly valuable for its treatment of the allegorical quality of the poem, though MacCallum may be thought now and then to push this too far.

MacEwen, V. *Knights of the Holy Eucharist.* London: Wells, Gardner, and Darton, 1912.

An interpretation of Tennyson's *Holy Grail* by a devout Anglo-Catholic Christian.

Maynadier, Howard. *The Arthur of the English Poets.* New York: Houghton Mifflin, 1907.

His purpose is "to select what seems to me the sanest of the frequently conflicting opinions of the Round Table stories which students of medieval literature have held, and to present them clearly, . . . to indicate the general tendencies of Arthurian literature in the English world from its first appearance to the present." The chapter on Tennyson, 410-438, is an excellent presentation of the appearance of the Arthurian story in his poetry and finally of the conclusion he reached in his treatment.

Miller, Betty. "Tennyson and the Sinful Queen," *The Twentieth Century,* CLVIII (October 1955), 355-363.

A Freudian interpretation which treats symbolically the conflict between sense and spirit in the universe. Controversial, provocative, and not always soundly based.

Nicoll, W. Robertson and Thomas J. Wise, ed. *Literary Anecdotes of the Nineteenth Century.* London: Hodder and Stoughton, 1895. Contributions towards a literary history of the period.

In Vol. II the chapter entitled, "The Building of the Idylls," 219-272, deals "exhaustively with an interesting and but little known subject, namely, the slow up-building and gradual development of Tennyson's *Idylls of the King* . . . the extent to which the Poet Laureate altered, re-wrote, revised, and recast the various portions of the work." The volume also includes miscellaneous Tennysoniana.

Pallen, Condé Benoist. "A Meaning of the *Idylls of the King*," *The Catholic World*, XLI (April 1885), 43-54.

Discusses intelligently the allegorical meaning of the *Idylls*, which had just appeared in their complete and final form.

Pallen, Condé Benoist. *Idylls of the King: an Essay in Interpretation*. New York: American Book Co., 1904.

An expansion of the article published in 1885 in the *Catholic World* (see preceding item)in respect of which the author received a commendatory letter from Tennyson. "I thank you for your critique on the *Idylls of the King*. You see further into their meaning than most of my commentators have done." Deserves careful study.

Poston, Lawrence. "The Argument of the Geraint-Enid Books in *Idylls of the King*," *Victorian Poetry* II, No. 4 (Autumn 1964), 269-275.

Here as elsewhere in the *Idylls* redemption is personal and the position of society ambiguous.

Priestley, F. E. L. "Tennyson's *Idylls*," *University of Toronto Quarterly*, XIX (October 1949), 35-49. In *Critical Essays*, ed. John Killham, pp. 239-255.

"The *Idylls* are so far from being escape that they represent one of Tennyson's most earnest and important efforts to deal with major problems of his time." Their real deficiency grows out of their piece-meal composition. A very valuable study.

Raybould, W. *Notes on Tennyson's 'Coming and Passing of Arthur.'* London: The Normal Press, 1907.

A useful booklet containing quotations from former critics and notes both explanatory and textual.

Reade, Willoughby. *Notes on the Arthurian Epic and on 'The Idylls of the King.'* Alexandria, Virginia: Willoughby Reade, Episcopal High School, 1908.

An excellent handbook for students, the main purpose being "to set forth certain facts concerning the Arthurian Epic in general and the Epic's latest setting, *The Idylls of the King*, in particular." A successful early attempt to give "the inner meaning of the *Idylls*, . . . particularly the parable and allegory which they contain."

Rowe, F. J. *The Coming of Arthur. The Passing of Arthur.* Ed. with Introduction and Notes. London: Macmillan, 1892. Uniform with G. C. Macaulay's editions of *The Marriage of Geraint* and *Geraint and Enid*, and *Gareth and Lynette*. A useful edition.

Ryals, Clyde de L. "The Moral Paradox of the Hero in the *Idylls of the King*," *E. L. H.*, XXX (March 1963), 53-69.
A scholarly and interesting interpretation of the *Idylls of the King*. It stands between the extreme abstract approach and the conventional interpretation; touches on the alien vision theme (see *The Alien Vision of Victorian Poetry* by E. D. H. Johnson); stresses the interpretation of self, will, love, reality, and man's need for props, either human or abstract. It is interesting to compare this 1963 point of view with that of J. M. Ludlow's "Moral Aspects of Mr. Tennyson's *Idylls of the King*," *Macmillan's Magazine*, I (November 1859).

Ryals, Clyde de L. "Percivale, Ambrosius, and the Method of Narration in *The Holy Grail*," *Die Neueren Sprachen*, XII (Jahrgang 1963), 533-543.
Interest lies in Mr. Ryal's interpretation of the character and function of Ambrosius in the grail idyll.

Shannon, Edgar F., Jr. "The Proofs of *Gareth and Lynette* in the Widener Collection," *Papers of the Bibliographical Society of America*, XLI (October 1947), 321-340.
Discusses in detail important corrected proofs and 97 holograph lines from the same poem bound up in same volume.

Smalley, Donald. "A New Look at Tennyson—and especially the *Idylls*," *Journal of English and Germanic Philology*, LXI, No. 2 (April 1962), 349-357.
A review of Jerome H. Buckley's *Tennyson* in which Professor Smalley makes a full and careful comparison of Buckley's views with those of Harold Nicolson and P. F. Baum.

Solomon, Stanley J. "Tennyson's Paradoxical King," *Victorian Poetry*, I, No. 4 (November 1963), 258-271.
Stresses the remarkable extent to which paradox, ambiguity and irony abound in *Idylls of the King*. A helpful essay.

Stevenson, The Rev. Morley. *Spiritual Teaching of the Holy Grail.* London: Wells, Gardner, and Darton, 1903.

A study of Tennyson's poem based on six Lenten addresses by the author.

Swinburne, Algernon Charles. *Under the Microscope.* London: D. White, 1872.

An attack on Alfred Austin's *Poetry of the Period*, containing Swinburne's famous criticism of *Idylls of the King*, "the Morte d'Albert as it might perhaps be more properly called."

Tennyson, Charles. "Tennyson Papers: III. *Idylls of the King*," *Cornhill Magazine*, CLIII, No. 917 (May 1936), 534-557.

Notes on the early manuscripts of the *Idylls of the King*, giving various readings and throwing "light on Tennyson's methods of composition."

Tennyson, Sir Charles. "*The Idylls of the King*," *The Twentieth Century*, CLXI (March 1957), 277-286.

Detailed account of the long-drawn-out composition of the *Idylls*. And see "Letter from Sir Charles Tennyson," *Twentieth Century* (April 1957), 393.

Turnbull, Arthur. *Life and Writings of Alfred, Lord Tennyson.* London and Felling-on-Tyne: The Walter Scott Publishing Co., 1914.

In his final chapter the author states as Tennyson's principal claim to greatness that "he is the fifth in succession to Virgil, Ariosto, Spenser and Milton to develop epic poetry into a new form." The *Idylls* "is the last product of a form of intellectualism which is passing away in favour of the drama and the modern novel, and Tennyson is its last poet." "This . . . is his place in the history of English literature, and in the literature of the world."

Wright, Herbert G. *Tennyson and Wales.* "Essays and Studies" by members of the English Association, XIV (1929), pp. 71-103. Oxford: Clarendon Press, 1929.

Briefly describes Tennyson's various visits to Wales and the effects of these on his poetry. Contains a detailed comparison of Tennyson's Geraint idylls with the glory in the *Mabinogion* on which they were founded.

12

Critical and Interpretative: Shorter Poems

DEMETER AND PERSEPHONE

Dahl, Curtis. "A Double Frame for Tennyson's *Demeter*," *Victorian Studies*, I (June 1958), 356-362.
Suggests that Tennyson's *Demeter* was in part answer to Swinburne's *Hymn to Proserpine*. Contains a useful summary of the relations between the two poets.

Kissane, James. "Victorian Mythology." See under *Critical and Interpretative, General*.

Stange, G. Robert. "Tennyson's Mythology: A Study of *Demeter and Persephone*," *E. L. H.*, XXI (March 1954), 67-80. In *Critical Essays*, ed. John Killham, pp. 137-150.
"The detached and almost hermetic quality of Tennyson's early poems did, it is true, give way to a tendency to homely didacticism, but the tension—and the richness—which mark the early work, can be found at the end as well as at the beginning of the collected poems." Here Tennyson has extended the meaning of the myth by grafting to it a hopeful vision of the future which embodies his conception of the gentle humanism of the Christian faith.

DESPAIR

Walker, Thomas. *Mr. Tennyson's "Despair."* London: Elliot Stock, 1883.
A discussion of Tennyson's poem by a Christian believer with special reference to the doctrine of Eternal Punishment.

A DREAM OF FAIR WOMEN

Shannon, Edgar F., Jr. "Tennyson's 'Balloon Stanzas,'" *Philological Quarterly*, XXXI (October 1952), 441-445.

Suggests that these stanzas, with which Tennyson's *A Dream of Fair Women* began when first published (*Poems, Chiefly Lyrical*) may have been based on a balloon ascent made from Cambridge on May 19, 1829, in which Tennyson's friend Richard Monckton Milnes took part.

ENOCH ARDEN

Bagehot, Walter. "Wordsworth, Tennyson, and Browning." See under *Critical and Interpretative, General*.

The British Controversialist. London: Houlston and Wright, 1865.

This monthly publication, apparently aimed at the serious and intelligent sections of the artisan and lower middle classes, contained, in the issues for January, February, March and April, articles affirmative and negative on the question, "Is Tennyson's *Enoch Arden* a poem morally objectionable?" These are interesting as showing how an important section of the new reading public approached literature.

HAIL, BRITON! and TITHON

Donahue, Mary Joan. "Tennyson's *Hail, Briton!* and *Tithon* in the Heath Manuscript," *PMLA*, LXIV (June 1949), 385-416.

The first part deals with an early poem of 50 stanzas in the *In Memoriam* metre which exists only in J. M. Heath's Commonplace Book in the Fitzwilliam Museum, Cambridge. Many stanzas and lines from this poem were used by Tennyson in later publications, but the poem itself was never published by him. It is of interest not only as illustrating his poetic technique, but also as throwing light on his views and thought during his Cambridge period.

The second part deals with an early version of *Tithonus*, also from J. M. Heath's *Commonplace Book*. The principal interest of this lies in the alterations and improvements made in the poem before it was published in 1860. Miss Donahue's treatment of both poems is thorough and illuminating and the essay deserves careful study.

Ricks, Christopher. "Tennyson's *Hail Briton* and *Tithon*: Some Corrections," *Review of English Studies*, N.S., XV (February 1964), 53-55.

Concerns texts of these two poems as transcribed by Miss M. J. Donahue in *PMLA*, LXIV (June 1949), 385-416. Raises various questions.

THE HESPERIDES

Stange, G. Robert. "Tennyson's Garden of Art: A Study of 'The Hesperides,'" *PMLA*, LXVII (September 1952), 732-743. In *Critical Essays*, ed. John Killham, pp. 99-112.

" 'The Hesperides' should help us to define Tennyson's poetic achievements. It is a complex and allusive work that makes brilliant use of metaphor and the language of paradox."

THE LADY OF SHALOTT

Packer, Lona Mask. "Sun and Shadow: The Nature of Experience in Tennyson's 'The Lady of Shalott,'" *Victorian Newsletter*, No. 25 (Spring 1964), 4-8.

A useful survey of current criticism, most of which deals with the poem as illustrating the antithetical nature of art and reality. The author's view is that reality, as it appears in the poem, has both a metaphysical orientation in Platonic dualism and a sexual content.

LOCKSLEY HALL

Bufkin, E. C. "Imagery in 'Locksley Hall,'" *Victorian Poetry*, II, No. 1 (Winter 1964), 21-28.

Defends Tennyson's poem against charges of incoherence. It shows the young protagonist standing in the present at a point of decision, then breaking away from the past and launching out into the future. This theme is unified by three different but not unrelated sets of imagery, based on time, water, and sky.

Templeman, William Darby. "A Consideration of the Fame of 'Locksley Hall,'" *Victorian Poetry* I, No. 2 (April 1963), 81-103.

Stresses the great weight of the contribution which *Locksley Hall* (1842) has made to the establishment and maintenance of Tennyson's hold upon the English-speaking public. "Possibly no other single poem ever written with fewer than two hundred lines has as impressive a record."

Templeman, William Darby. "Tennyson's 'Locksley Hall' and Thomas Carlyle," *Booker Memorial Studies: Eight Essays on Victorian Literature in Memory of John Manning Booker, 1881-1948*, ed. Hill Shine. Chapel Hill: University of North Carolina Press, 1950, pp. 34-59.

"Purpose (1) to increase the interest of at least one famous poem, 'Locksley Hall,' (2) to provide new indication of Tennyson's poetic skill, and (3) to strengthen and increase one's appreciation of the great influence wielded by Thomas Carlyle." Templeman takes as his thesis the idea that 'Locksley Hall' is Tennyson's translation of *Sartor Resartus*, Book II.

LOCKSLEY HALL SIXTY YEARS AFTER

Gladstone, W. E. "'Locksley Hall' and the Jubilee," *The Nineteenth Century*, XXI (January 1887), 1-18.

Gladstone's review of "Locksley Hall Sixty Years After" clearly shows his alarm and distress at the pessimism of Tennyson's poem. Gladstone gives an impressive catalogue of the reforms adopted by Parliament since 1842 (the date of the publication of the first "Locksley Hall" and maintains that the second "Locksley Hall" is purely subjective, the poet's imagery being like the perception of colour by the eye, which tells only the individual's impression of the thing seen.

THE LOTOS-EATERS

Grob, Alan. "Tennyson's 'The Lotos-Eaters': Two Versions of Art," *Modern Philology*, LXII (November 1964), 118-129.

Compares the poem with Tennyson's "The Hesperides," "The Lady of Shalott" and "The Palace of Art" and traces in the alterations made by the poet between 1832 and 1842, the effect of his gradual conversion from a purely aesthetic to a social view of the poet's function.

Maclaren, Malcolm. "Tennyson's Epicurean Lotos-Eaters," *Classical Journal*, LVI (March 1960), 259-267.

Discusses the Epicurean references of Tennyson's poem. Rejects the views of critics who depreciate the poem's intellectual content. "It is not the work of a great creative intellect, but it has intellectual overtones which are considerable, and it demands intellectual equipment on the part of its readers for its full understanding."

Marshall, George O., Jr. "Tennyson's 'The Lotos-Eaters': An Essay Toward Appreciation," *Creativity and the Arts*, ed. George O. Marshall, Jr. Athens: University of Georgia Center for Continuing Education, 1961, pp. 35-45.

An excellent presentation. It gives suggestions as to sources of the poem, form and technique, theme and revision.

LUCRETIUS

Buckler, William E. "Tennyson's 'Lucretius' Bowdlerized?" *Review of English Studies*, N.S., V (July 1954), 269-271.
Argues that the "bowdlerization" of the poem for publication in *Macmillan's Magazine* was for literary rather than Mrs. Grundyish reasons.

Jebb, R. C. "On Mr. Tennyson's 'Lucretius,'" *Macmillan's Magazine*, XVIII (June 1868), 97-103.
An analysis and commentary on 'Lucretius' by an able scholar.

MAUD

Howe, M. L. "Rossetti's Comments on 'Maud,'" *Modern Language Notes*, XLIX (May 1934), 291.
Contains some passages in letters from Rossetti to William Allingham, omitted from the printed edition of the Rossetti's letters. Of interest critically and biographically.

Johnson, Edward Dudley Hume. "The Lily and the Rose: Symbolic Meaning in Tennyson's 'Maud,'" *PMLA*, LXIV (December 1949), 1222-1227.
Suggests that throughout his poem Tennyson uses the lily as the symbol of purity or modesty, and the rose as a symbol of passion, and that Tennyson stands in very much closer relation to the symbolist tradition in poetry than is generally realized. A brief essay but thorough and ingenious. Has been very influential.

Killham, John. "Tennyson's 'Maud,'" in *Critical Essays on the Poetry of Tennyson*, ed. John Killham, pp. 219-235. London: Athlone Press, 1960.
Deals effectively with the function of the imagery in the poem. Its theme is "the attainment through sexual love of a psychic balance," its meaning is "diffused through its individual lyrics and monologues, each of which seeks to portray in words a singular human experience." A thorough and illuminating study.

Kirkwood, Kenneth Parker. *'Maud'—An Essay on Tennyson's Poem*. Ottawa: Le Droit, 1951.

A long essay of over 200 pages discussing Tennyson's poem from biographical, critical, psychological, and other angles.

Mann, R. J. *Tennyson's 'Maud' Vindicated*. London: Jarrold and Sons, 1856,

A 78 page study of Tennyson's poem, defending it against the almost universal depreciation with which its publication in 1855 had been greeted. Considering the difficulty and novelty of 'Maud,' Mann's understanding both of its technique and true objects is remarkable. The essay received the expressed approval of Tennyson himself. See *Memoir*, I, 405-406.

Marshall, George O., Jr. "Tennyson's 'Oh! That 'Twere Possible': A Link between *In Memoriam* and 'Maud,' " *PMLA*, LXXVIII (June 1963), 225-229.

By using the John Moore Heath commonplace book, now in the Fitzwilliam Museum in Cambridge, Mr. Marshall traces Tennyson's reworking of 110 lines beginning 'Oh! that 'twere possible,' 1837, and the much longer passage in "Maud," 1855. He then uses the theme as a link between *In Memoriam* and "Maud."

Rader, Ralph Wilson. "The Composition of Tennyson's '*Maud*,' " *Modern Philology*, LIX (May 1962), 265-269.

A convincing argument concerning the composition of "Maud," differing from the "often retold story of how Tennyson came to write 'Maud.' " The essay appears as Section I of Chapter I of Rader's *Tennyson's 'Maud': The Biographical Genesis*.

Ryals, Clyde de L. "Tennyson's 'Maud,' " *Connotation*, I (Spring 1962), 12-32.

A very interesting essay. Emphasizes that "the real artistic unity of 'Maud' lies not in the fact that the drama unfolds through the senses of one man, but in the fact that in all its overlapping levels of meaning the drama creates from its complexity a greater whole." Interesting comparison with Eliot's "Waste Land."

Stokes, Edward. "The Metrics of 'Maud,' " *Victorian Poetry*, II, No. 2 (Spring 1964), 97-110.

After a full and interesting analysis the author concludes, " 'Maud' remains one of the most remarkable pieces of metrical resourcefulness in English poetry."

MERLIN AND THE GLEAM

Haight, Gordon S. "Tennyson's 'Merlin,'" *Studies in Philology*, XLIV (July 1947), 549-566.
Theme stressed is that of the autobiographical value of "Merlin and the Gleam."

THE PALACE OF ART

Howell, A. C. "Tennyson's 'Palace of Art'—An Interpretation," *Studies in Philology*, XXXIII (July 1936), 507-522.
The essay suggests, not very convincingly though with much detailed argument, that one object of the poem was to allegorize the pedantry and remoteness of the scholar's life at Cambridge in Tennyson's time.

SIR GALAHAD

Donahue, Mary Joan. "The Revision of Tennyson's 'Sir Galahad,'" *Philological Quarterly*, XXVIII (April 1949), 326-329.
Based on an early version of the poem in J. M. Heath's Commonplace Book, now in the Fitzwilliam Museum, Cambridge. Interesting as illustrating Tennyson's method of work.

TEARS, IDLE TEARS

Assad, Thomas J. "Tennyson's 'Tears, Idle Tears,'" *Tulane Studies in English*, XIII (1963), 71-83.
A valuable study of the prosody, structure, and meaning of Tennyson's poem.

Brooks, Cleanth. "The Motivation of Tennyson's Weeper," *The Well Wrought Urn: Studies in the Structure of Poetry*. New York: Reynal, 1947. In *Critical Essays*, ed. John Killham, pp. 177-185.
An interpretation of "Tears, Idle Tears."

Hough, Graham. "'Tears, Idle Tears,'" *Hopkins Review*, IV (1951), 31-36. In *Critical Essays*, ed. John Killham, pp. 186-191.
Tennyson's greatest successes "again and again are found to lie in his power of taking an extremely vague and unspecific and objectless emotion, and giving it form, not indeed by intellectualizing it, but by embodying it, partly in images, partly in sound-patterns, of which he is one of the greatest masters in the language." See also F. W. Bateson, *Romantic Schizophrenia*, under *Critical and Interpretative: General*.

Spitzer, Leo. " 'Tears, Idle Tears' Again," *Hopkins Review*, V (1952), 71-80. In *Critical Essays*, ed. John Killham, pp. 192-203. Disagrees with Graham Hough's interpretation. Compares the treatment by Ovid, Quevedo, Tennyson, Hofmannsthal and Hemingway of the fear of approaching death.

THE TWO VOICES

Brashear, William R. "Tennyson's Third Voice," *Victorian Poetry*, II (Autumn 1964), 283-286.

The essay deals with Tennyson's "The Two Voices" and points out that in addition to the still small voice which urges the poet to suicide, and that of the poet which attempts to rebut its arguments, there is a third voice which only appears at the end and which succeeds in rescuing the self from suicide. The writer identifies this with the "living will" of "In Memoriam" 131.

ULYSSES

Bush, Douglas. "Tennyson's 'Ulysses' and *Hamlet*," *Modern Language Review*, XXXVIII (January 1943), 38.

Calls attention to an echo in Tennyson's poem, "How dull it is to pause," of Hamlet's soliloquy in Act IV, iv, 32 ff.

Chiasson, E. J. "Tennyson's 'Ulysses'—a Reinterpretation," *University of Toronto Quarterly*, XXIII (July 1954), 402-409. In *Critical Essays*, ed. John Killham, pp. 164-178.

Chiasson discusses the views of P. F. Baum and C. C. Walcutt on this poem and advances his own interpretation.

Marshall, George O., Jr. "Tennyson's 'Ulysses,' " *The Explicator*, XXI (February 1963), Item 50.

A vindication of Ulysses's attitude towards his son, Telemachus. Opposes interpretation of Baum, *Tennyson Sixty Years After*, and Chiasson in *University of Toronto Quarterly*, XXIII, 1954.

Mitchell, Charles. "The Undying Will of Tennyson's 'Ulysses,' " *Victorian Poetry* II (Spring 1964). 87-95.

A valuable contribution to the discussion of this important poem. The poem is not a dramatic monologue. It is a soliloquy in the form of a dramatic address which implies action. The voyage for which Ulysses is preparing is the act of dying and his goal is spiritual reality.

SHORTER POEMS 93

Pettigrew, John. "Tennyson's 'Ulysses': A Reconciliation of Opposites," *Victorian Poetry*, I, No. 1 (January 1963), 27-45.

Perhaps no Victorian poem packs such an infinity of riches into as little room as "Ulysses." The author finds the poem "considerably more comprehensive and complex" than earlier critics have done.

Robson, W. W. "The Dilemma of Tennyson," *Listener*, June 13, 1957, pp. 936-965. In *Critical Essays*, ed. John Killham, pp. 155-163.

Sums up the "incongruity" of the poem "Ulysses" thus: "Tennyson, the responsible social being, the admirably serious and 'committed' Victorian intellectual, is uttering strenuous sentiments in the accent of Tennyson, the most unstrenuous, lonely and poignant of poets." Yet the poem remains very beautiful and, in its way, perfect. Detects a gradual breakdown between Tennyson's "art" and his "social conscience."

Roppen, Georg. " 'Ulysses' and Tennyson's Sea-Quest," *English Studies*, XL (April 1959), 77-90.

A useful analysis, the conclusion of which is that "Ulysses" effects, better than any other of Tennyson's poems of quest, an imaginative reconciliation of the perplexities of 'The Two Voices' and *In Memoriam*."

Schell, E. A. "Tennyson's 'Ulysses,' " *Methodist Review*, XCV (March/April 1913), 192-202.

A very eulogistic, though carefully compiled, study. Interesting contrast to more analytical modern criticism.

Stanford, W. B. *The Ulysses Theme*. Oxford: Blackwell, 1954.

A comprehensive study of the poetic treatment of Ulysses from Homer onwards. Tennyson's "Ulysses" is discussed on pp. 232-234. Worth study.

Walcutt, C. C. "Tennyson's 'Ulysses,' " *Explicator*, IV (February 1946), Item 28.

Detects a dichotomy between Tennyson's own account of his meaning and "the desolate melancholy music of the words themselves."

Note: See also P. F. Baum in *Tennyson, Sixty Years After* and an excellent discussion of "Ulysses" in Edgar Hill Duncan's "Tennyson: a Modern Appraisal" (both under *Critical and Interpretative, General*).

13

Tennyson and the Reviewers

Cruse, Amy. *The Victorians and Their Books*. London: Allen and Unwin, 1935.
   Contains some interesting details regarding the effect of Tennyson's poetry on his contemporary readers.

Eidson, John Olin. *Charles Stearns Wheeler: Friend of Emerson*. Athens: University of Georgia Press, 1951.
   Gives more details of the support given to Tennyson during the 1830's and 1840's by literary circles in New England.

Eidson, John Olin. *Tennyson in America: His Reputation and Influence from 1827-1858*. Athens: University of Georgia Press, 1943.
   A very complete study, scholarly and interesting. Treats influence of Tennyson on American poets and critics, and the influence of American criticism upon Tennyson. Another link in the chain of speculation concerning the influence of the reviewers upon the development of Tennyson's art and personality.

Green, Joyce. "Tennyson's Development During the 'Ten Years' Silence' (1832-1842)," *PMLA*, LXVI (September 1951), 662-697.
   A brilliant analysis of Tennyson's reaction to the reviewers and to the world about him. The Appendix contains "tables [which] record the numbers and nature of the strictures applied to those poems which Tennyson subsequently revised, and his reaction to individual reviewers." Should be read with E. F. Shannon's *Tennyson and the Reviewers*.

Marchand, Leslie A. *The Athenaeum, a Mirror of Victorian Culture*. Chapel Hill: The University of North Carolina Press, 1941.
   Throws interesting light on contemporary critical reactions to Tennyson throughout his life.

Paden, W. D. "Tennyson and the Reviewers (1829-1835)," in *Studies in English in Honor of Raphael Dorman O'Leary and Selden Lincoln Whitcomb*, ed. Lawrence: University of Kansas Humanities Studies, 1940.

A full and valuable study, elaborating many of the points taken by Edgar F. Shannon and Joyce Green, q. v.

Shannon, Edgar F., Jr. "The Critical Reception of Tennyson's 'Maud,'" *PMLA*, LXVIII (June 1953), 397-417.

The essay attempts to determine as accurately as possible the critical reactions to "Maud" and also to examine its effect upon Tennyson's revision of the poem and upon his decision to proceed with the *Idylls of the King*. The treatment is full and judicious and an appendix contains a valuable bibliography of reviews and articles during the years 1855-1859.

Shannon, Edgar F., Jr. *Tennyson and the Reviewers*. Cambridge: Harvard University Press, 1952.

The purpose of this important study is to trace the growth of Tennyson's reputation in the British Isles from 1827 through 1851 and to show the extent to which the opinions of the reviewers influenced the actual writing of his poetry. Chief reliance is placed on the periodical press of the time, but reference is also made to letters, diaries, and biographies of prominent figures of the period and to remarks in books published between 1834-1852. Should be read with Joyce Green's study.

14

The Dramas

Archer, William. *English Dramatists of Today*. London: Sampson, Low and Co., 1882.
   Pages 334-351 deal with Tennyson's first four plays. Interesting as the criticism of an intelligent and practical man of the theatre. Believes that "under proper conditions *Queen Mary* might become a most valuable addition to the acting drama of England. *Harold* presents as great opportunities as *Queen Mary* and casting should not prove nearly so difficult, and surely we may hope one day or other to see it worthily placed upon the stage." Considers *The Falcon* much superior to *The Cup*.

Block, Louis J. "The Dramatic Sentiment and Tennyson's Plays," *Poet-Lore*, VIII (October-November 1896), 512-527.
   Challenges the general depreciation of Tennyson's plays, maintaining that they attempt "in the genuine modern manner" to go beyond merely depicting action, and to depict the real springs of action in the historical times of which they treat.

Dickinson, Thomas H. *The Contemporary Drama in England*. London: John Murray, 1920.
   Pages 27-29 deal with Tennyson and dismiss his plays as significant only in showing "his possession in old age of a fecund and experimenting mind." They "have the appearance of mechanical exercises in an imitated art."

"The Dramas of Alfred Tennyson," Anon. rev., *Edinburgh Review*, CXLV (April 1877), 383-415.
   Reviewing *Queen Mary* and *Harold*. Refers both dramas to the class of dramas intended for reading only. Goes through both plays in detail. Finds that *Queen Mary* has no climax and aims at no result. "That the poem exhibits no little pathos and power of indicating character in certain scenes is unquestionable; but that it should be spoken of as a model of dramatic force only shows what contemporary dramatic criticism has

come to." The writer finds the construction of *Harold* much better but is compelled to hold the play unsuccessful. It is conceived epically rather than dramatically and "pervaded by a fatal self-consciousness."

Eidson, John Olin. "The Reception of Tennyson's Plays in America," *Philological Quarterly*, XXXV (October 1956), 435-443.
A useful summary of the reception by American critics of Tennyson's plays. In spite of the successful runs enjoyed by *Queen Mary*, *Becket* and *The Foresters* on the American stage, and the favourable reaction of one or two leading critics, Professor Eidson considers that in the history of Tennyson's reputation in America the plays must be regarded as liabilities.

Eidson, John Olin. "Tennyson's Minor Plays in America," *American Notes and Queries*, IV, No. 2 (October 1965), 19-21.
Deals with the American reception of *The Falcon*, *The Cup*, and *The Promise of May*. Though this note was published after December 31, 1964, it is included as supplying information not elsewhere available.

Granville-Barker, Harley. "Tennyson, Swinburne, Meredith— and the Theatre," *The Eighteen-Seventies: Essays, by Fellows of the Royal Society of Literature*, ed. Harley Granville-Barker, pp. 161-191. Cambridge: Cambridge University Press, 1929.
A favourable analysis of Tennyson's *Queen Mary* but also a fair discussion of the points at which Tennyson failed as a dramatist, by an actor, producer, dramatist and dramatic critic of outstanding ability.

James, Henry. "Tennyson's Drama," *Views and Reviews*. Boston: Ball Publishing Co., 1908.
Deals with *Queen Mary* and *Harold* as originally published. A most acute and sympathetic survey of Tennyson's achievement as a poet. Finds that *Queen Mary's* fundamental weakness is that it has no really dramatic subject or form. "The temper of the poem is so noble that the critic who has indulged in a few strictures as to matters of form feels as if he had been frivolous and niggardly . . . though it is not the best of a great poet's achievement, only a great poet could have written it." James is much less favourable to *Harold*, finding it "not in the least bad: it contains nothing ridiculous, unreasonable or disagreeable; it is only decidedly weak, colourless and tame. . . .

Harold would be a respectable production for a writer who had spent his career in producing the same sort of thing, but it is a somewhat graceless anomaly in the record of a poet whose verse has, in a large degree, become part of the civilization of his day." One of the most valuable studies of Tennyson yet written, though limited by the writer's purely aesthetic approach.

Japikse, Cornelia G. H. *The Dramas of Alfred, Lord Tennyson.* London: Macmillan, 1926.

Based on a thesis written for the University of Amsterdam. A useful though perhaps not very penetrating work. Contains a valuable summary of contemporary criticism and a good survey of Tennyson's sources. The author's conclusion is that, although for depth of thought and beauty of expression the dramas contain some of Tennyson's finest work, from a dramatic standpoint they do not, except *Harold*, fully satisfy the demands of the stage. The dramatic element is undoubtedly present, but sometimes, as in *Queen Mary*, obscured by a too much divided interest.

Nicoll, Allardyce. *A History of Late Nineteenth Century Drama: 1850-1900.* Cambridge: Cambridge University Press, 1949.

Pages 258-259 deal with Tennyson's plays. *Queen Mary* has a good theme and a wretched handling; *Harold* seems monotonously pretentious; and *Becket* is fogged in Tennyson's most dignified gloom. True he won a certain measure of success on the stage, but that was due to combination of the author's poetic fame and the equally popular acting of Irving and the Kendals.

See also: H. B. Cotterill, "*The Cup*" *by Alfred, Lord Tenneyson* under "*The Cup* and *The Falcon:* Publication."

Note: Critical accounts of Tennyson's career as a dramatist will be found in the standard biographies and volumes of general criticism, e.g. *Tennyson, A Memoir* by Hallam, Lord Tennyson (Macmillan, 1897); *Alfred Tennyson* by Charles Tennyson (Macmillan, 1949); *Tennyson: The Growth of a Poet* by Jerome H. Buckley (Harvard University Press, 1960); *Tennyson* by Morton Luce (Dent, 1901); *Tennyson Laureate* by Valerie Pitt (Barrie and Rockliff, 1962); *The Pre-Eminent Victorian* by Joanna Richardson (Jonathan Cape, 1962); *A Tennyson Handbook* by George O. Marshall (Twayne Publishers Inc. 1963). Relevant material will also be found in *Henry Irving* by Laurence Irving (Faber and Faber, 1961);

Personal Reminiscences of Henry Irving by Bram Stokes (Heineman, 1906); *The Story of My Life* by Ellen Terry (Hutchinson and Co., 1908); *A Few Memories* by Mary Anderson (Osgood Mellwarne, 1896); and *The Life of Augustin Daly* by J. F. Daly (Macmillan, 1907).

"Special Despatch to the *Herald* by Cable. London, April 22, 1876." Anon. rev., *New York Herald* (April 23, 1876), 7.

A detailed description filling 3½ columns concerning the production, acting, scenery, and costliness, with a valuable account of the immense interest in literary and dramatic London and of Tennyson's eagerness to succeed on the stage.

"Tennyson as Dramatist," Anon. rev., *Academy*, LII, August 14, 1897, pp. 134-135.

Notes general failure of modern poets as dramatists. Tennyson's equipment for dramatic writing inferior to Browning's. Such success as he achieved was due as much to actors and producers as to himself.

Queen Mary

Publication

Brody, G. M. *Tennyson's "Queen Mary": A Criticism.* Edinburgh: MacLachlan and Stewart 1895. London: Simpkin, Marshall and Co., 1875.

A long and detailed attack on Tennyson's play. "We have tried the drama by the accredited standard, and we find it wanting." Worth study and consideration.

[Jebb, R. C.] "Notes on Mr. Tennyson's *Queen Mary*," *Macmillan's Magazine*, XXXII (September 1875), 434-441.

Anonymous, but in fact by Professor R. C. Jebb; a learned and careful review by a first-class scholar. Dealing with the criticism that Mary is not a fit subject for tragedy, Jebb makes the pertinent reply that Tennyson's subject is not Mary but England. He praises the character drawing, but notes the occasional suspension of interest through the poet's too careful study of historical facts. In conclusion Jebb notes with interest that the play is said to be much admired by Walt Whitman.

Lang, A. "*Queen Mary*," *Academy*, June 26, 1875, pp. 649-650.

A review by Andrew Lang, an eminent and versatile Victorian *litterateur*, of the published play. Finds the subject too monotonous and depressing for tragedy. Emphasizes the masterly elaboration of the minor characters. *Queen Mary* is full of various interest and insight: it shows powers unguessed at and as yet scarcely to be appreciated.

"Mr. Tennyson's Drama," Anon. rev., *The Spectator,* June 26, 1875, p. 820.

This review does not say that *Queen Mary* is Tennyson's best work, but that it is among his best works. It is "strong from end to end, thoroughly dramatic, characters clearly defined." The greater part of the review is given to character analysis.

"*Queen Mary,*" Anon. rev., *The Athenaum,* July 3, 1875, p. 13. Second notice.

A good part of the review is given to a comparison of the characters of Elizabeth and Mary. Songs are quoted and important bits of dialogue which reveal character, especially that of the cruel Philip. The reviewer closes with regret that "the Laureate has deserted the ground in which his strength lay to make an experiment in the drama." He considers *Queen Mary* unsuited to the stage.

"*Queen Mary,*" Anon. rev., *The Saturday Review,* July 3, 1875, p. 19.

First half of rather long review is given to the faults of the drama; last part praises certain passages. Concludes that "the whole effect is disappointing, and the impression which it leaves upon the reader's mind is one of a dreary and bitter harshness."

"*Queen Mary,*" Anon rev., *The Times*, June 19, 1875, p. 12.

Not only a fine poem but a fine drama. Has a dramatic fire last found in a comparably vivid historical embodiment in Shakespeare's *Henry V*. Review covers a column and a half, praises the narrative passages and the humorous prose dialogue. (In fact by R. C. Jebb.)

"*Queen Mary:* A Drama," Anon. rev., *Church Times,* July 2, 1875, p. 330.

The reviewer does not feel that Mary's story justifies dramatic presentation. He considers certain scenes dramatic, but the entire article centres on the failure here of the dramatic form.

"*Queen Mary:* A Drama," Anon. rev., *The Guardian,* June 30, 1875, p. 837.

A very intelligent review in which the author evaluates practically every aspect of the drama and reaches no dogmatic conclusion. Instead he suggests points for consideration. Worth studying.

"*Queen Mary:* A Drama," Anon. rev., *Midland Counties Herald*, June 24, 1875, Supp. p. 1.
Very short review, no quotes, but interesting comment.

"*Queen Mary:* A Drama by Alfred, Lord Tennyson," Anon. rev., *The Anthenaeum*, June 26, 1875, pp. 845-848.
A first notice of the published volume. Finds that although as a drama it lacks all essentially dramatic quality and fails to stir or to rouse, it is nonetheless a work of serious purpose and sustained effort. It is difficult to image a study more exact and sincere than that of *Queen Mary*, but there is never that collision of interest or feud of motive which are necessary to true drama.

"Recent Literature," Anon. rev., *Atlantic Monthly*, XXXVI (August 1875), 240-241.
A review of the newly issued volume, *Queen Mary*. Notes the looseness of structure, capricious changes of scene, vast spaces of time and place, the roughness and unfinish of certain verses, and the broken verses Elizabethanly scattered through the play. Tennyson's experiment cannot be considered successful in a dramatic or high poetical sense.

"Tennyson's *Queen Mary*," Anon. rev., *Nonconformist*, June 23, 1875, p. 639.
Queen Mary abounds in "delicate phrasing, gems of thought, rare grasp of character, a broad masterly conception of the period, a rare vein of humour. . . . Mr. Tennyson has kept close to history." The essence of the dramatic conception lies in his making Mary's bigotry and cruelty cause her to lose Philip, whose love she would secure.

"Tennyson's *Queen Mary*," Anon. rev., *Quarterly Review*, CXXXIX (July 1895), 231-248.
Queen Mary a literary drama, below the dignity of a truly great stage. Action is subordinated to idea; subtle analysis substituted for active imagination; motive exhibited rather than effected; the best specimen of this literary drama written in our time—at least admirable in form. Of the dramatic spirit, in the Shakespearean sense, it has nothing. But as an intellectual

exercise . . . a monument of ingenious and refined expression . . . it may long continue to give pleasure to the reader.

See also under "*Dramas—General*"
 Archer, William. *English Dramatists of Today.*
 "The Dramas of Alfred Tennyson," *Edinburgh Review,* CXLV (April 1877), 883.
 Granville-Barker, Harley. "Tennyson, Swinburne, Meredith and The Theatre."
 James, Henry. "Tennyson's Drama."
 Japikse, Cornelia G. H. *The Dramas of Alfred, Lord Tennyson.*

Production

Eidson, John Olin. "Tennyson's First Play on the American Stage," *American Literature,* XXXV, No. 4 (January 1964), 519-528.
 Describes the very successful production of Tennyson's *Queen Mary* by an Irish actress, Augusta Dargon, in various parts of America during the years 1875-1878. No copy of the adaptation used by Miss Dargon seems to exist.

Irving, Laurence. *Henry Irving.* London: Faber and Faber, 1951.
 Pp. 264-267 and 274-275 contain some account of the production and some criticism of the play.

"Lyceum," Anon. rev., *Daily News,* April 19, 1876, p. 2.
 Review of the Lyceum's production. "Owing to the cuts, *Queen Mary* becomes little more than a bigoted lady, rather foolishly fond of a cruel husband." But the play was produced "with a success which few even of the poet's admirers could have hoped for a dramatic poem so wanting in the stirring action which audiences are accustomed to expect in a historical play."

"Our London Cable Letter," Anon. rev., *New York Herald,* April 23, 1876, pp. 7,10.
 Discusses the cutting of the long drama for stage presentation. Interesting account of the Laureate's "frequent appearances at the stage door of the Lyceum" as probably "so many efforts to procure a commutation of the sentence of death upon so many of his characters and their lines." But concludes "the Laureate in a sensible man."

"*Queen Mary,*" Anon. rev., *Pall Mall Gazette,* April 20, 1876, p. 11.

Review of the Lyceum production. Finds that the play presents few of the all but essential conditions of dramatic success. The repulsive, bigoted, and lovesick Mary cannot sustain the interest of the piece and her cold hard husband cannot afford the relief we seek.

"*Queen Mary* at the Lyceum," Anon. rev., *Academy*, April 22, 1876, p. 392.

Praises the conciseness and restraint of the writing but asks "where was the concentration and continuity of interest in a play to be played?" Points out how many of the strongest episodes and characters of the printed play have had to be omitted. The weak acting of some of the minor characters robbed the play of much of its effect, though one or two of the parts were acted as well as they could be. Criticizes the acting of both Mary and Elizabeth.

"*Queen Mary* at the Lyceum," Anon. rev., *The Era*, April 23, 1876, p. 12.

Criticizes the adaptation for omitting Cranner, Wyatt, and Cardinal Pole. The play is destitute of action and frequently robbed of all meaning. Irving's comedy the sole relief to the dullness of the whole.

"*Queen Mary* at the Lyceum," Anon. rev., *The Times*, April 20, 1876, p. 7.

A dramatic poem, not in the truest sense a drama. Criticizes the adaptation. There is far more action in the published poem than in the play. If *Queen Mary* could have been put on the stage in its original form it would have done the poet much more credit and had much more chance of securing a permanent place in the national repertory.

Anon. rev., *Standard*, April 19, 1876, p. 3.

Queen Mary not written for the stage; a historical narrative in dramatic form. In portrayal of character entirely successful, but nothing is brought about that the audience desires to see, nor is interest or sympathy strongly enlisted in support of anyone. Though not an exciting play, contains much to gratify the audience. Criticizes the omissions but praises the acting of Irving and Miss Bateman.

"Tennyson's *Queen Mary*," Anon. rev., *The Era*, April 16, 1876, p. 10.

Judging from Mr. Tennyson's earlier works no one would have imagined him capable of giving so much picturesque effect and so much dramatic significance to the subject-matter which he has chosen for his play. Criticizes Tennyson for giving the theme a purely feminine interest which draws attention away from the public actions involved.

"Tennyson's Drama on the Stage," Anon. rev., *Spectator*, April 22, 1876, p. 526.
A review of the Lyceum production of *Queen Mary*. Criticizes the adaptation of Tennyson's play which omits the most effective situations. Also strongly attacks Miss Bateman's acting of the name part. "But with all its defects there is so much in the play as given at the Lyceum to give the effect of a great dramatic history, that we should not be surprised to find it growing, instead of dwindling, in favour."

Harold

PUBLICATION

[Jebb, R. C.] *The Times*, December 18, 1876, p. 6.
Tennyson proves that he can do justice to the great historical events which group themselves with a tragic distinctness around Harold. The studies of character are carefully and subtly finished. A larger, freer atmosphere, more action and above all more sunshine than in *Queen Mary*. The review fills three and a quarter columns and analyzes the play in detail.

"*Harold: A Drama*," Anon, rev., *The Academy*, January 6, 1877, p. 1.
Considers Harold a subject far more dramatic than Queen Mary. An historical play, *Harold* derives its movement from the evolution of events. "A real drama in its continuity of motion." Evaluates the characters portrayed.

See also under *Dramas-General:*
Archer, William, *English Dramatists of Today*.
"The Dramas of Alfred Tennyson," *Edinburgh Review*, CXLV (April 1877), 383-415.
James, Henry. "Tennyson's Drama," *Views and Reviews*.

PRODUCTION

Birrell, Francis, "The Court Theatre: *Harold* by Alfred, Lord Tennyson," *Nation*, April 14, 1928, p. 45.
A very intelligent and sophisticated review of the Court Theatre production. *Harold* is less obviously dramatic and full-

blooded than *Queen Mary*, nevertheless far from being a languid *pastiche*. The production often childishly ineffective and at least one character, Wulfnoth, "turned into a drivelling idiot." The verse reaches a high general level . . . with fragmentary outbursts of high poetry, so "Lord Tennyson got through on his own merits." Play has faults. Tennyson copies his Elizabethan ancestors too closely and "The nationalist self-satisfaction of the conclusion, 'Make them one people,— Norman, English,' knocks the bottom out of the drama."

"Drama. Harold," Anon. rev., *New Age*, April 12, 1928, p. 285.

"As a drama the play shows a great many amusing faults . . . to balance its faults, *Harold* is written in vigorous, full-sounding verse . . . the most interesting aspect of the play being the antithesis between the self assurance in this present day of psychological self-probing. . . . The production takes the play as an opportunity for a literary pageant; as an occasion for declaiming and setting heroic verse."

Eidson, John Olin. "The First Performance of Tennyson's *Harold*," *The New England Quarterly*, XXXVII, No. 3 (September 1964), 387-390.

An excellent account of the first performance of *Harold*, June 19, 1915, by the Yale University Dramatic Association in New Haven, Connecticut. Article also includes summaries of the American reviews of the production. Professor Eidson is the leading American authority on Tennyson's dramas.

"*Harold* at The Royal Court Theatre," Anon. rev., *The Era*, April 11, 1928, p. 6.

Many stirring scenes, a great deal of the verse very fine indeed. Some scenes stand out as compellingly interesting. Action lacks continuity. Characters interesting but lack real breath of life. No touch of humour.

"*Harold* by Alfred, Lord Tennyson," *The Times*, April 3, 1928, p. 14.

Review of the Court Theatre production. The review may be summarized as follows: The narrative never falls into the shadow of monotony, but it never emerges into the full light of poetic imagination. It is not dull—a tale one is compelled eagerly to follow, but it never takes fire. The language is rich and distinguished, the order of relation admirable. The play is good, so that we are bound to admire it and take pleasure in it, but it is polite and withdrawn.

H. M. W. "The Royal Court Theatre," *Daily Telegraph*, April 3, 1928, p. 7.

Very favourable account of the production. Notes "rapt stillness" of the audience, "abounding English quality of the play, the language, and the acting. . . . The production is one which every student of our dramatic literature should on no account miss seeing."

Hutton, W. H. "Two Unfamiliar Plays," *Church Quarterly Review*, III (January 1931), 314-327.

Contains a reminiscence of the 1928 production at the Royal Court Theatre, London. Considers Tennyson's defect as a dramatic poet to be that he is too scanty in his poetry, which he sacrifices to dialogue. The acting showed that the play has real and vivid passages of fine drama and that it runs smoothly and quickly, with a real development and a coherent interest.

Jennings, Richard. "*Harold* by Alfred, Lord Tennyson at the Court Theatre," *Spectator*, April 14, 1928, p. 563.

"There is a faint life in *Harold*—we are glad to have seen him, though we feel that we do not want to see him too soon again." The experiment was worth making.

Macdonell, A. G. "*Harold*, by Alfred, Lord Tennyson (Royal Court)," *London Mercury*, XVIII (May, 1928), 87.

Review of the Royal Court Theatre production. An extremely interesting play; really a piece for the stage and not a rigmarole in blank verse—proves that Tennyson knew more about human emotions and passions than some of his poems would lead one to think. Also that although he knew very little about making his characters talk intelligently and intelligibly, he knew a dramatic situation when he saw one, and how to make use of it. Praises Tennyson's conception of Harold's character.

S. R. L. "Revival of *Harold*," *Morning Post*, April 3, 1928, p. 12.

"The play a weariness. One felt all the time that Tennyson was just 'yawning it out' in conscientious verse form." Commends the love scenes between Harold and Edith as having real beauty.

T. "At the Play. *Harold* (Royal Court)," *Punch, or the London Charivari*, April 11, 1928, p. 414.

Evaluates character portrayal and closes with a general summary. "*Harold* may be said to have antiquarian rather than dramatic interest. There were undeniable stretches of dullness; but there were at least occasional flashes of true fire; there was always something pleasant to look upon, and there were two jokes."

Becket

PUBLICATION

"Becket," Anon. rev., *The Athenaeum*, January 3, 1885, pp. 7-9.
   Concerned mainly with Becket's character. "What was it that impelled Becket suddenly to veer round and become the Church's most potent arm in its struggle with the Norman feudality?" Places "this tragedy very high in the dramatic poetry of this century."

"*Becket*," Anon. rev., *Spectator*, December 20, 1884, p. 1699.
   Criticizes the lack of adequate connection between the Becket element and the Fair Rosamund story. Compares Tennyson's play unfavourably with Aubrey de Vere's *St. Thomas of Canterbury* in many respects, but concludes, "certainly amongst the works by which Tennyson will be always remembered, *Becket* will rank as one, though not amongst the highest and the most perfect. It has the stamp of true power upon it, and often unquestionable dramatic power too."

"*Becket* by Alfred, Lord Tennyson," Anon, rev., *The Athenaeum* January 3, 1885, p. 7.
   A review of the published volume. While criticizing Tennyson's statement of the cause of the quarrel between Becket and the King and the introduction of the Fair Rosamund, admits that the Rosamund scenes are a great success and her character most beautiful and winning, while Becket's is most vigorous and masculine. "On the whole, indeed, we cannot err in placing this tragedy very high in the dramatic poetry of this century."

Dierickx, J. "King and Archbishop: Henry II and Becket, from Tennyson to Fry," *Revue des Langues Vivantes*, XXVIII (1962), pp. 424-435.
   A full comparison of Eliot and Fry, touches Tennyson's play very briefly, referring to its "coloured, confused, romantic picture," use of historical-legendary material and complicated plot. "It is common knowledge that the success of Tennyson's

plays depend rather on the magnetic personality and theatrical talent of Irving than on the dramatic skill of the author." An examination of *Becket* suggests that Irving's talent must have been great indeed.

Egan, M. F. "St. Thomas of Canterbury and Becket," *Catholic World*, XLII (December 1885), 382-395.

Compares Tennyson's play very unfavourably with Aubrey de Vere's *Thomas of Canterbury*. The writer's opinion is largely conditioned by religious considerations, which reduce its critical value.

Egan, M. F. "Imitators of Shakespeare," *The Ghost in Hamlet*. Chicago: A. C. McClurg, 1906.

Contrasts Tennyson's *Becket* unfavourably with Aubrey de Vere's *Thomas of Canterbury*, while classing both as closet dramas. The author was evidently a Catholic and to some extent prejudiced by his dislike of Tennyson's characterization of Becket. He ignores the theatrical success of Irving's production. Some of his criticism no doubt well founded.

"English History on the Stage," Anon. rev., *Pall Mall Gazette*, December 9, 1884, p. 1.

Main idea is that since "the people of England are entering into the inheritance of English history," the Laureate's play is timely.

Hawkins, Frederick. "Becket," *The Theatre*, V (February 1885), 53-61.

Finds the published play deficient in action, variety, picturesqueness, and other essential qualities of an acting play, but sees compensations in the lofty and far reaching conception of the chief figures and the high literary standard.

Lambert, Agnes. "The Real Thomas Becket," *Nineteenth Century*, XXXIII (February 1893), 273-292.

A survey of recent research and estimates of Becket with a study of Tennyson's play which acclaims it as his noblest work.

"Lord Tennyson's *Becket*," Anon. rev., *Macmillan's Magazine*. LI (February 1885), 287-294.

A full and careful study, placing Tennyson's dramatic work in the sequence of his development. Expresses the wish that Tennyson had given more of Becket the Chancellor, so as to emphasize and explain the change in his attitude. By implication but not expressly, the reviewer dislikes the introduction of the Rosamund story. Thinks that the last act would make a great effect on the stage. Whether or not *Becket* ever reaches the stage, it was worth Tennyson's writing, and is worth reading.

"Lord Tennyson's Definition of a King," Anon. rev., *The Present Day*, II (January 1885), 61.
By the use of quotations selected from the play, the critic presents Tennyson's definition of a King, the central idea being a "description of the calamities which come of a feeble maintenance of just law and order."

Mackail, J. W. "Becket," *Academy*, December 27, 1884, pp. 421-422.
"It does not seem probable that Lord Tennyson will be known by his drama to future ages." The drama has "more tragic depth than *Harold* and deals with a nobler character than *Mary*." Stresses great improvement in Tennyson's dramatic verse, expressing the opinion that it is the best since Shakespeare. As the play was not written for the stage, Tennyson might have given fuller rein to the more purely poetic quality of his writing. In spite of defects (such as the infelicitous prose humour), *Becket* is entitled to take rank as a great play and worthy of its author. A considered criticism by a fine scholar.

"Lord Tennyson's *Becket*," Anon. rev., *St. James's Gazette*, December 9, 1884, p. 11.
Quotes and discusses main scenes that centre on Henry II, Queen Eleanor, Rosamund, Clifford, and Becket.

"Lord Tennyson's *Becket*," Anon rev., *St. James's Gazette*, December 12, 1884, p. 10.
"Apropos of the Laureate's new poem, *The Athenaeum* reproduces the following estimate of it by Mr. G. H. Lewes, who read it some years ago. 'A kaleidoscope of lovely, wise and humorous fragments is constantly shifting before my mind's eye, and I try to piece them into a whole and to reread the noble work. But many readings will be necessary. For it is only a vain critic who does not know by trial what a work of art is, who can decide on a first inspection of what has cost the artist years of thought and rejections. The critic too often thrusts forward the suggestion which the artist early saw and rejected. The play is instinct with dramatic life and

is as various as Shakespeare, and (unlike Shakespeare) nowhere is there any fine writing thrust in because it is fine, and because the poet wanted to say the fine things that arose in his mind. . . . I have no hesitation in saying that, however the critics of tomorrow will unanimously declare Alfred Tennyson to be a great dramatic genius.'"

"Lord Tennyson's *Becket*," Anon. rev., *St. James's Gazette*, December 31, 1884, p. 6.

Considers *Becket* a "dramatic poem rather than a drama. . . . He reproduces in poetical garb a profoundly interesting episode in English history, the struggle between Church and State in the twelfth century." Concludes that "*Becket* will always rank with the very best of Lord Tennyson's work."

"Lord Tennyson's New Play," Anon. rev., *The Times*, December 10, 1884, pp. 5-6.

"Lord Tennyson is no antiquarian dramatist. Like Shakespeare he takes a broad and familiar outline and uses it for a dramatic purpose. His object is to write a play, not to rewrite history. . . . *Becket* is a work eminently worthy of Lord Tennyson's genius and fame. It is dramatic in its conception and execution, full of poetry and fire; its versification is strong and varied in cadence, and its several episodes are well conceived and skillfully woven together."

"Lord Tennyson's *Becket*," Anon. rev., *The Standard*, December 9, 1884, p. 5.

The critic feels that the play is about Fair Rosamund rather than Thomas à Becket. "Many scenes are dramatic, not in form only, but also and above all in spirit. . . . From a stage point of view, Lord Tennyson's poem presents two centres of interest: Rosamund visited by Queen Eleanor in the Bower and the scene of Becket's murder." Demonstration is made of how the two centers of interest interweave. Attention is also called to the "famous chess scene." Long quotations are given from the play.

Rehak, Louise Rouse. "On the Use of Martyrs: Tennyson and Eliot on Thomas Becket," *University of Toronto Quarterly*, XXXIII (October 1963), 43-60.

An interesting and full study, which concludes, "*Murder in the Cathedral*, Eliot's best play, remains outside the meaning of our tradition of drama . . . it is a message play in the way Shaw's message plays are not. Tennyson's human sympathies

THE DRAMAS 111

are wider, if his theatrical sense is less developed . . . it has something of our current flavour of the drama of alienation in its ironic texture of relationships. It is still enjoyable literature, if it is not the finest Tennyson."

"Tennyson's *Becket*," Anon. rev., *Saturday Review*, December 15, 1884, p. 757.
Criticizes the introduction of the Rosamund episode, and of Walter Map and Margery. "On the whole, though *Becket* fails of the aim which its author would reach, it is a work which will sustain his claim as a fine thinker, with a grand perception of what is noblest in human character." It will not advance Lord Tennyson's claim to rank among the great tragedians in England."

PRODUCTION

(The acting version of the play prepared by Irving is printed in the relevant volume of the *Eversley Edition of Tennyson's Works*, pp. 427-526.)

A. B. W. [Arthur Bingham Walkley]. "*Becket*," *The Speaker*, February 11, 1893, pp. 157-158.
Walkley objects to the method of other critics who pick the play to pieces instead of truthfully representing the actual impression made by the production. He admits and indicates the play's many faults, but "the great point is that the play as presented at the Lyceum is alive with colour, movement and humanity." Walkley was, with William Archer, one of the two leading dramatic critics of the period.

"*Becket*," Anon. rev., *The Critic*, November 18, 1893, p. 326.
Review of Irving's production in New York. "An illustration of what can be done with second-rate dramatic material by the aid of really good stage-management and a well-trained company." Emphasizes Tennyson's ignorance of theatrical requirements and the skill of Irving's adaptation, and the excellence of the mounting and of Irving's acting.

"*Becket* at the Lyceum," Anon. rev., *Daily News*, February 7, 1893, p. 3.
A long laudatory review of the Lyceum production, emphasizing the strong hold which the play exercised over the audience and the splendour of mounting and presentation. Little criticism of the play itself.

"*Becket* at the Lyceum," Anon. rev., *The Era*, February 11, 1893, p. 10.

"Here is a story in places reaching the heights and sounding the depths of passion and pathos . . . in the end presenting us with a tragedy as powerful and awe-inspiring as any the stage has known. It held the rapt attention of the house from first to last."

"*Becket* at the Lyceum," Anon. rev., *Morning Post*, February 7, 1893, p. 5.

A long notice speaking enthusiastically of Irving's production and acting and giving a full outline of the story, but saying little about Tennyson's contribution to the immense success of the evening.

"*Becket* at the Lyceum," Anon. rev., *Pall Mall Gazette*, February 7, 1893, pp. 1-2.

Tennyson's "plays are never good plays. Perhaps the worst of them all is *Becket*. Nothing can make it dramatic, nothing can lend it life." But the writer praises Irving's acting unreservedly, and rather inconsistently finds his Becket the best thing he has done since his Philip in *Queen Mary* in 1876.

"Becket at the Lyceum," Anon. rev., *Saturday Review*, February 11, 1893, p. 146.

The success of *Becket* on the stage is the success not of a great play but of a play brilliantly illustrated by the resources of an accomplished master of stagecraft, and by the services of an actor and of an actress who at their best have no rivals on our stage. Criticizes the irrelevancy of the Rosamund and Eleanor episodes to the main subject.

"*Becket* at the Lyceum," Anon. rev., *Spectator*, February 25, 1893, p. 253.

Tennyson has seized the genius of Becket's character and Mr. Irving has seized the genius of Tennyson's idea. Taken altogether the play is not without considerable defects as an acting play; but the central figure and incidents are most nobly conceived, and are presented in a manner worthy of their conception.

Eidson, John O. "Tennyson's *Becket* on the American Stage," *The Emerson Society Quarterly*, XXXIX (Quarter II, 1965), 18-20.

"Irving's stage-version of *Becket* did more than anything else toward giving Tennyson the name of dramatist which he so ardently desired, and the tremendous acclaim given the 69 performances in America were a big help." Prof. Eidson gives a summary of the American reviews and a brief account of Irving's various tours with the play in the U. S. A.

Irving, Laurence. *Henry Irving*. London: Faber and Faber, 1951.
Pages 554-562 contain a most valuable account of Irving's production, of his reverential opinion of the play and of its importance in his repertoire during the last years of his life. An account is given of the command performance at Windsor before Queen Victoria on March 18, 1893.

"Lyceum: *Becket*, a Drama in a Prologue and Four Acts, by Alfred, Lord Tennyson," Anon. rev., *The Athenaeum*, February 11, 1893, pp. 193-4.
Finds the play shapelier and comelier and losing none of its strength through the cuts made from the printed text. Welcomes especially the disappearance of Walter Map, "the most ponderous and ineffective example of comic interest since the days of Milton." The early scenes are inspiring, the later solemn and impressive. Irving's Becket a genuine revelation.

"Lyceum Theatre," Anon. rev., *The Times*, February 7, 1893, p. 7.
Approves the adaptation, in terms suggesting that the critic did not quite realize the amount of omissions. "*Becket* cannot, without reservations, be described as a masterpiece." The author has not "attempted to lay bare the springs of action, human and personal, in his characters." Sympathy with the King detracts from the interest in the Archbishop. It is not clear whether the latter is intended to be a sympathetic character or not.

"Mr. Irving's Production of *Becket* at the Lyceum," Anon. rev., *Manchester Guardian*, February 7, 1893, p. 7.
"Mr. Irving was not only audible in every syllable he uttered, but also found in Becket one of the most impressive characters he has ever presented. . . . It cannot be said that the Rosamund and Eleanor episode comes out very effectively. On the other hand the scenes in which Becket is mainly concerned are found to be impressive in the highest degree."

"Tennyson's *Becket* at the Lyceum Theatre," Anon. rev., *Daily Telegraph*, February 7, 1893, p. 6.
A two-column review of Irving's production. Emphasizes the great popular success of the first night. Defends the inter-

weaving of the Rosamund story. Is *Becket* a great play? It has good moments—Prologue effective, First Act grand, then a decline. Love-making, humour not very effective. Lyrical passages have all the witchery of Tennyson's touch and many scenes by no means wanting in dignity and power. Time alone can solve the question of the play's status.

Wedmore, Frederick. "Tennyson's *Becket*," *Academy*, February 18, 1893, pp. 158-159.

Scarcely an inspired utterance, yet it has fine scenes, fine passages and from beginning to end scholarly and delicate treatment. The language, if not often exalted, has generally the merit of directness and simplicity, and at need it does acquire elevation. The writer emphasizes the play's great popular success, but evidently thinks this largely due to Irving's acting and production. Becket a most finished picture.

The Cup and *The Falcon*

Production

"Contemporary Verse," Anon. rev., *The Times*, May 5, 1884, p. 3.

The Cup both easier to read and to act than *The Falcon*. Refers to some passages from *The Cup* as being "by this time too well known to need quotation." Comments on the combination of literary and dramatic ability, rare in modern times. The subject of *The Falcon* inadequate to the dramatic form chosen by Tennyson and repulsive in itself to English feeling. "A much more artfully constructed piece could with difficulty support the linked humours long drawn out of Filippo and his mother."

Cotterill, H. B. *The Cup by Alfred, Lord Tennyson.* With Introduction and Notes. London: Macmillan and Co., 1903.

Thirteen pages of biographical introduction, some errors of fact. Fifteen introductory pages about the play. Full and useful notes. The author regards the question of Tennyson's merit as a dramatist as being still *sub judice*. The plays are the work of a poet, containing many passages of imagination, power and splendid diction, and some of the characters have the power of engaging our interest or our affections, although perhaps only gradually, as is sometime the case in real life.

THE DRAMAS 115

"*The Cup* and *The Falcon*," Anon. rev., *The Athenaeum*, March 8, 1834, p. 319.
An elaborate and well informed survey of the history and current status of the poetic drama. It is not easy to assess the writer's opinion of Tennyson's plays.

"*The Cup* and *The Falcon*," Anon rev., *Spectator*, March 8, 1884, p. 316.
The Cup described as "one of the most remarkable of the Laureate's minor efforts. Tragedy is seldom compressed within limits so narrow as these, seldom outlined in strokes so few and yet so effective . . . what the Poet Laureate has done so powerfully in *The Cup* he seems to us to have failed to do in *The Falcon* to be as faint and poor an outline as we hold *The Cup* to be powerful and effective."

"*The Cup* and *The Falcon*," Anon. rev., *Yorkshire Illustrated Monthly*, May 1884, pp. 343-349.
Both plays very slight in form and there is nothing deep or striking in them. . . . "Tennyson has not the grasp of character, the intense insight into human nature nor the power of putting himself *into* his characters which are absolute essentials in a dramatist."

Morshead, E. D. A. "*The Cup* and *The Falcon*," *Academy*, March 8, 1884, pp. 160-161.
Regrets the compression of *The Cup* into two short acts and the consequent insubstantiality of the characters. But the play, though thinly and slightly worked out, is substantial and robust compared to *The Falcon*.

PRODUCTION: *The Cup*

"*The Cup* at the Lyceum," Anon. rev., *Saturday Review*, January 8, 1881, p. 48.
"Has an amount of dramatic force which may not have been expected." Finds the second act much less dramatic than the first. Praises very highly Ellen Terry's performance, which reveals her as a great actress.

"Lyceum Theatre," Anon. rev., *The Morning Post*, January 4, 1881, p. 5.
"The plot never flags for a moment. There are no digressions, or unreasonable descriptions, or long speeches. Every sentence carries the action forward. The interest, profoundly

tragic from the first, deepens as it proceeds." Praises the production.

"The New Drama of the Laureate," Anon. rev., *Pall Mall Gazette*, January 5, 1881, p. 10.

The writer finds, as in the performance of a Greek tragedy or an Elizabethan masque, a complete concourse of the arts. "As illustration of heroic action and accompaniment of heroic speech, comes every known form of picturesque or musical accessory, and a spectacle is supplied which at the same time satisfies the senses and stimulates the imagination." Without being dramatic in the strict sense of the word, the play is tragic in amplitude of idea and in power and severity of style. "So sparing is the use of any form of poetic adornment, that the play from the literary standpoint remains apart from any previous work of its author."

"The Lyceum Theatre," Anon. rev., *The Times*, January 5, 1881, p. 4.

Finds the play an advance on *The Falcon*. Things are done on the stage and not merely talked about. Emphasizes the magnificence of the production and the excellence of the acting, particularly of Ellen Terry in the central figure, but finds something shadowy and unreal in the whole work, whether that of actors or author.

"Mr. Tennyson's Play at the Lyceum," Anon. rev., *Spectator*, January 15, 1881, p. 81.

Complains that either the author or lessee have forbidden publication of the text, so that quotation is impossible. "The educated Englishman who misses seeing *The Cup* misses an intellectual enjoyment such as is rarely offered to him—he loses an hour and a half of total self-forgetfulness." An enthusiastic notice, describing the story as "antique and solemn and bare as if related by the author of the *Book of Kings*."

"Mr. Tennyson's Tragedy at the Lyceum," Anon. rev., *The Standard*, January 4, 1881, p. 3.

"*The Cup* is the production of a keen and competent playwright as well as of a poet." Rather full account of staging. Compliments the stage management, Miss Terry and Mr. Irving.

"Mr. Tennyson's New Play at the Lyceum," Anon. rev., *Daily News*, January 4, 1881, p. 6.

THE DRAMAS

"That the play itself is pleasing we cannot affirm. The keynote is mournful, its incidents even approach the repulsive, and its moral teaching hardly comes within the sympathies of modern audiences." The author has given full prominence to the painful features of the story and even scorned to furnish them with anything in the shape of relief."

"Mr. Tennyson's New Play," Anon. rev., *The Daily Telegraph*, January 4, 1881, p. 3.

Begins with historical background of the play. Gives quotations and outline of the story, followed by rather long analysis of details. Review is of value.

"Tennyson's New Play," Anon. rev., *The Era*, January 8, 1881, p. 5.

Praises setting and acting enthusiastically. An artistic triumph, likely to attract and delight cultivated playgoers for a considerable time. The Play, though not boasting too much action for the amount of text, is yet a great advance on *The Falcon*. Its simple, tragic story lays firm hold of the interest from the outset and there are many passages replete with poetic beauty.

Wedmore, Frederick. "Mr. Tennyson's New Play," *Academy*, January 8, 1881, pp. 34-36.

The play has no interest through elaboration of plot or development of character. There are no contrasting humours of secondary characters, no marked subtlety of thought, but a powerful story is strongly handled. Opportunity is provided for fine acting and scenic display. The play does not humbly accompany the spectacle. The spectacle splendidly illustrates the play.

PRODUCTION: *The Falcon*

"The Poet Laureate's New Play," Anon. rev., *The Era*, December 21, 1879, p. 6.

An acted poem rather than a play. Elevation of sentiment, purity and nobleness of style. Praises lighting, dresses, and scenery.

"Mr. Tennyson's New Play," Anon rev., *Pall Mall Gazette*, December 31, 1879, p. 12.

Finds the story unfit for dramatic treatment. To make it inoffensive it has to be made ineffective. With all the play's beauty of workmanship and dramatic skill it leaves the audience cold, in spite of the music of the verse, the felicities of expression, and the dignity and nobility of thought.

"Mr. Alfred Tennyson's New Play," Anon. rev., *Standard*, December 19, 1879, p. 3.

Mr. Tennyson possesses the dramatic instinct in a marked degree, but to show this on the boards is very different from showing it in a poem. Though many speeches forcible, little action to relieve the dialogue. *The Falcon* so short that the spectator, carried away by the beauty of the verse and the legend, has not time to note absence of action. Does not like Filippo. "There is so much to be grateful for in this tender and pathetic idyll that one must not venture to criticize slight faults. The effect of such a play can only be to purify and elevate the English Theatre."

"The Stage," Anon. rev., *Academy*, January 3, 1880, p. 18.

Refers to "pleasant lines of Tennysonian simplicity and Tennysonian terseness," but neither poetical nor dramatic excellence appears and some broader comedy introduced into the piece gave little pleasure to the audience.

"St. James's Theatre," Anon. rev., *Daily Telegraph*, December 19, 1879, p. 3.

The play, though overcharged with sorrow, is both graceful and pretty. The verse will fall with pleasure on the musical ear. Not so much a play as a picture of great beauty relieved by recitation.

"St. James's Theatre," Anon. rev., *Morning Post*, December 19, 1879, p. 5.

Brilliant and accurate spectacle. A tender, graceful idea clothed in nervous verse singularly free from needless ornament. "A touching and admirable little piece in which dramatic shortcoming is scarcely evident." The management of the St. James has done itself high honour in this production.

"St. James Theatre," Anon. rev., *The Times*, December 20, 1879, p. 11.

Work not unworthy of the poet's fame. Many eloquent and graceful passages. Praises dresses and scenery. The action not represented but related. Must rank among those plays which are no plays. The Kendals not able to express the poetical, so fail to give the characters reality.

The Promise of May

Production

" 'Locksley Hall Sixty Years After' by Alfred, Lord Tennyson," Anon. rev., *Athenaeum*, January 1, 1887, p. 31.

In a review of this volume the critic deals briefly with *The Promise of May*. Finds this "the outcome of a polemical rather than an artistic impluse." Nevertheless in the time of Robson and what was called "Domestic Melodrama" it could have been exactly in touch with a London audience.

"Tennyson's New Poems," Anon. rev., *Spectator*, December 25, 1886, pp. 1750-1751.

Deals with *The Promise of May*. Though this did not succeed and was not likely to succeed on the stage, it would be impossible not to speak of it with respect as a poem. "It is the fruit not the root of evil that can be made dramatic, and Tennyson spends comparatively little of his genius on the fruit, and much upon the germs."

Publication

Archer, William. *About the Theatre*. London: T. Fisher Unwin, 1886.

Pp. 81-88 contain an interesting account of the production of Tennyson's *The Promise of May*. Archer was the leading dramatic critic of the late 19th century and a devotee of Ibsen.

Daily News, Anon. rev., November 13, 1882, p. 2.

Contains a very full description of the first night of *The Promise of May* and its disastrous reception. "The truth is that the author . . . has failed because he has proceeded upon an essentially undramatic method."

"The Globe. *The Promise of May*," Anon. rev., *The Era*, November 18, 1882, p. 6.

Refers to the play's "weakness, its crudeness, its ill construction, its preachiness, its lack of interest, its unreality, its want of action." The audience assembled "prepared to admire, but remained to scoff."

"The Globe," Anon. rev., *The Times*, November 13, 1882, p. 6.

Finds the motive of the play essentially undramatic. The play has neither plot nor situation. "As a poem the grim story . . . might have been developed into a decent *Manfred*. As a play the best fate to be hoped for it is that it should be speedily forgotten."

"Mr. Tennyson's Play," Anon. rev., *Saturday Review*, November 18, 1882, p. 670.

"*The Promise of May*, unhappily, has nothing that for stage purposes can be called incident, and is lamentably deficient in any true exposition of character." Edgar comes out both unintelligible and undramatic, a creature whose amazing actions are supposed to be explained by the talk which is both amazing and dull.

"Mr. Tennyson's *Promise of May*," Anon. rev., *Pall Mall Gazette*, November 13, 1882, p. 4.

"Illogical in assumption, undramatic in treatment, prosaic in detail, and all but unrelieved by any grace of fancy, this feeble and illjudged protest against modern agnosticism brings on its author, at an age when for most men the tumult of conflict is over, his first signal defeat."

"Tennyson as Dramatist," Anon. rev., *Spectator*, November 18, 1882, pp. 1474-1475.

"A very acute critic of great experience, who was present at the Globe on one of the nights of its performance, said . . . that everything in it which ought to have been said out straight, was left to be implied, and everything which ought to have been left to be implied, was said out straight. . . . Tennyson habitually unravels action into thought and feeling, rather than weaves thought and feeling into action. This is why he is so little fitted for the production of stage drama."

Tennyson, Lionel. "Edgar in *The Promise of May*," *Daily News* (n.d.), quoted at length on p. 1008 of the annotated edition of Tennyson's works issued by Macmillan & Co. in 1913.

"Edgar is not as the critics will have it, a freethinker drawn into crime by his Communistic theories; Edgar is not even an honest Radical, not a sincere follower of Schopenhauer; he is nothing thorough and nothing sincere. He has no conscience until he is brought face to face with the consequences of his crime, and in the awakening of that conscience the poet has manifested his fullest and subtlest strength." A thorough analysis of Edgar's character follows. This exploration, written by his son, may be assumed to represent the poet's intentions.

Wedmore, Frederick. "Tennyson's Play," *Academy*, November 18, 1882, pp. 370-371.

THE DRAMAS   121

While emphasizing the play's obvious and fatal defects, suggests that the homeliness and tenderness of *The Promise of May* might yet effectively charm if abridged into one long act lasting about an hour.

The Foresters

Production

"*The Foresters*," Anon. rev., *Saturday Review*, April 2, 1892, pp. 391-392.

"The only unfavourable remark which we can conceive as uttered by a critic even if he were carpingly given, after a first reading of *The Foresters*, is 'rather slight', and we are pretty sure that a second would, in the case of a good critic, modify this at least to the extent of 'perhaps not so slight after all'. . . . The real merit of this piece lies in the way in which dialogue and songs, plot and characters, are co-ordinated in the presentation of this 'Forest life.'"

"*The Foresters*, Lord Tennyson's New Drama," Anon. rev., *Birmingham Gazette*, March 29, 1892, p. 4.

Approves the author's attention to customs and modes of speech, which transport the reader back to the time of Robin Hood. Says Tennyson has done for Sherwood Forest what Shakespeare did for Arden.

"The Laureate's *Foresters*," Anon. rev., *Globe*, March 29, 1892, p. 3.

Calls *The Foresters* a sylvan comedy; spirit of *As You Like It* and *A Midsummer Night's Dream*. "Thoroughly English characters, landscape, tone. Breezy in style and atmosphere, redolent of the wild wood and the wild life therein." Prose as masterfully handled as the verse. General result is pleasing and impressive.

"Lord Tennyson's New Play," Anon. rev., *Daily News*, March 29, 1892, p. 2.

Says *The Foresters* has no great dramatic action but is alive from first to last. Notes similarities to *As You Like It* and *Ivanhoe*.

"Lord Tennyson's New Drama," Anon. rev., *Glasgow Herald*, March 29, 1892, p. 4.

Closing statement: "The drama is full of choice poetical passages, and the characters of Robin Hood and Maid Marian are powerfully drawn."

"Lord Tennyson's New Poem," Anon. rev., *The Manchester Examiner*, March 30, 1892, p. 5.
Gives short account of the story. Notes "no deep seriousness, no moral lesson, beautiful wording and delicate fancy. . . . Villains and good characters held in contrast . . . excellent for reading."

"Lord Tennyson's New Poem," Anon. rev., *The Manchester Guardian*, March 29, 1892, p. 5.
Gives analysis of Tennyson's use of the Maid Marian legend. Calls the drama "a pastoral dramatic sketch. No elaborate dramatic character-drawing or elaborate dramatic story . . . charm of the piece is in succession of bright and cheerful scenes, decked with snatches of song." Lyric note is uppermost; emphasis on songs. A long review.

"Tennyson's Forest Idyll," Anon. rev., *The Christian Herald*, March 31, 1892, p. 6.
Praises the poet's understanding and presentation of England's heroic past, and use of legend.

PRODUCTION

"Alfred Tennyson's Play at Daly's," Anon. rev., *World*, March 18, 1892, p. 10.
Calls *The Foresters* "a delicate and poetical comedy; much of its effectiveness due to Sullivan's music." Gives a list of notable persons who saw "a notable first production," and who came to "have the ear charmed by classical phrases and gossamer-like melody." Notable names: Charles Dudley Warner, W. D. Howells, Edison Booth, Cornelius Vanderbilt. Interesting discussion of the production.

Daly, Joseph Francis. *The Life of Augustin Daly*. New York: Macmillan, 1927.
Contains a full account of Daly's production of *The Foresters* in New York and London.

Eidson, John Olin. "Tennyson's *The Foresters* on the American Stage," *Philological Quarterly*, XLIII, No. 4 (October 1964), 549-557.

THE DRAMAS 123

A very full account of Daly's negotiations with Tennyson and the production of *The Foresters:* first the successful year in America, opening March 17, 1892 and running until April 23 in New York; then on tour to Washington, Baltimore, Boston, San Francisco. Then the second opening in New York on January 24, 1893—all a great success with Arthur Sullivan, Daly, Ada Rehan, John Drew combination. Mr. Eidson gives content of American reviews and closes with an explanation of the play's failure in London in October, 1893.

"*The Foresters*," Anon. rev., *The Critic*, March 26, 1892, p. 186.
Review of Daly's New York production. There can be no doubt that the representation, upon the whole, was successful, but what proportion of credit for this result is due to the Laureate and what to the manager is another question. Stresses the charm of the writing and Tennyson's "curious lack of dramatic insight and . . . evidently unconscious defiance of all laws of construction and probability."

"*The Foresters:* Robin Hood and Maid Marian by Alfred, Lord Tennyson, Poet Laureate," Anon. rev., *Athenaeum*, April 16, 1892, pp. 491-492.
"A careful and discriminating study of the Robin Hood Ballads has gone to the composing of this lovely play." Play has enjoyed great success in America. We shall look forward with impatience to seeing it acted on English boards. The Americans seem to be ahead of British audiences in acceptance of drama as a literary form. *The Foresters* is a picture play. Characters part of the scene, and could hardly exist apart from it. Comparison with Thomas Hardy's *Under the Greenwood Tree*. Plot purposely slight and intensity of the interest and passion purposely kept down.

"Lord Tennyson's *Foresters* at Daly's Pleases the Public," Anon. rev., *Commercial Advertiser*, March 18, 1892.
"It is poetic and picturesque." Success as a dramatist, for which Tennyson longed, came after his eightieth year. The review speaks of the idyllic charm, beauty of the settings, the music, lyrics, the fairy scene in the third act. The play "secured an undoubted success." Audience also cheered Mr. Daly for his production of the play.

"Lord Tennyson's New Play," Anon. rev., *The Daily Graphic*, April 2, 1892, p. 439.
Praises the American production at Daly's in New York. Says the play is constructed with a greater regard for the

stage than any other of the poet's dramas. "It is shorter, it is less overcrowded with characters; the speeches are kept within the right and reasonable limits of theatrical declamation." More practical but less dramatic than *Harold* or *Queen Mary*.

"Lord Tennyson's Play," Anon. rev., *The Times*, March 19, 1892, p. 7.
"*The Foresters* a notable success at Daly's. The most delightful first night of the season—Ada Reham's triumph as Maid Marian—John Drew as Robin Hood. . . . There never was a more successful first night at Daly's Theatre."

Addendum

ARTHUR HENRY HALLAM

Pearce, Helen. "Homage to Arthur Henry Hallam," in *The Image of the Work*. Essays in criticism by B. H. Lehman and others. Berkeley: University of California Press, 1955, pp. 113-133.

A carefully reasoned study of Hallam's essay on some of the characteristics of modern poetry, and on the lyrical poems of Alfred Tennyson, published in *The Englishman's Magazine*, August, 1831.

TENNYSON AND SCIENCE

Millhauser, Milton. *Just Before Darwin*. Middletown, Connecticut: Wesleyan University Press, 1958.

ANNOTATED EDITIONS AND SELECTIONS

Woods, George Benjamin, and Jerome Hamilton Buckley, eds. *Poetry of the Victorian Period*. New York: Scott, Foresman, 1955.

The introduction is worth study.

CRITICAL AND INTERPRETATIVE: GENERAL

Buckley, Jerome H. *The Victorian Temper: A Study in Literary Culture*. Cambridge: Harvard University Press, 1951.

Chapter IV deals with Tennyson and foreshadows the views expanded in Buckley's biography of the poet.

Krause, Anna. "Unamuno and Tennyson," *Comparative Literature*, VIII (April 1956), 130-135.

Analyzes philosophic concepts common to both poets.

Smith, Elton Edward. *The Two Voices: A Tennyson Study*. Lincoln: University of Nebraska Press, 1964.

A valuable and concentrated study. The author deplores the insistence of modern criticism upon "the fragmentation and partition" of Tennyson's poetry and explains the apparent ambivalence which marks so much of it, by a detailed examination of five major tensions which, he considers, affected the poet throughout his long career: (1) Art versus Society, (2) Sense versus Soul, (3) Doubt versus Faith, (4) Past versus Present, (5) Delicacy versus Strength.

In Memoriam

Burchell, Samuel C. "Tennyson's Dark Night," *South Atlantic Quarterly*, LIV (January 1955), p. 75.

Stresses and analyzes the great influence which *In Memoriam* exercised on the Victorian Era and the decline of his reputation during the first third of the 20th century.

Fairchild, Hoxie Neale. *Religious Trends in English Poetry: 1830-1880*. New York: Columbia University Press, 1957.

Part IV deals with Tennyson. Worth study.

Fox Adam. "Tennyson's Elegy," *Spectator*, June 16, 1950, pp. 816-817.

A sympathetic critic makes one or two useful points.

9-18-68
MBK